Autistic World Domination

of related interest

An Adult with an Autism Diagnosis
A Guide for the Newly Diagnosed
Gillan Drew
ISBN 978 1 78592 246 6
eISBN 978 1 78450 530 1

Nerdy, Shy, and, Socially Inappropriate
A User Guide to an Asperger Life
Cynthia Kim
ISBN 978 1 84905 757 8
eISBN 978 0 85700 949 4

AUTISTIC
WORLD DOMINATION

How to Script Your Life

Jolene Stockman

Jessica Kingsley Publishers
London and Philadelphia

First published in Great Britain in 2023 by Jessica Kingsley Publishers
An imprint of Hodder & Stoughton Ltd
An Hachette UK Company

1

A CIP catalogue record for this title is available from the
British Library and the Library of Congress

ISBN 978 1 83997 444 1
eISBN 978 1 83997 445 8

Printed and bound in Great Britain by Clays Ltd

Jessica Kingsley Publishers' policy is to use papers that are natural,
renewable and recyclable products and made from wood grown in
sustainable forests. The logging and manufacturing processes are expected
to conform to the environmental regulations of the country of origin.

Jessica Kingsley Publishers
Carmelite House
50 Victoria Embankment
London EC4Y 0DZ

www.jkp.com

Contents

From Jolene

People love telling autistics what we can't do. Our limitations and weaknesses. How we are disordered, how we are deficient. There are entire industries working to fix us, people paid to train us, research us, to find subtle (and not so subtle) ways to yeet us from the planet. It is everywhere and it is boring. Being autistic often means being painfully aware of the ways we don't fit. And guess what? We don't need a book to remind us of our limitations – the whole world does that. Many of us exist under huge physical, mental, and emotional exhaustion. Many of us are underemployed, financially disadvantaged, adrift from family, lonely and demoralized after years of fighting systems, people, and places that are not designed for us. There is staggering privilege that comes with being born into a welcoming world, and if that's you? Sit down. This book aims to bring autistics what we truly need: respect, fierce optimism, and practical strategies that light the way.

The word *domination* oozes power and control. However, the word actually comes from the Latin *dominus* meaning master of a household. So, we're not here to boot out the neurotypicals, colonize the system, or gobble up the resources for ourselves (although finding some middle ground would be ideal). We're here to master ourselves, our spaces, and to make the world our home. And maybe for me that means cutting back on social interactions and shopping online. And maybe for you it means putting yourself out there and building independence. But for all of us it means letting go of trying to be like anyone else, trying to exist for or as anyone else. We belong in this world, and we deserve joy, peace, and success – however that looks for us.

Introduction: We are on the same planet, but not in the same world

We tell ourselves there is a normal, that we come in the same packages of meat and bones, capable of the same things. But there is no normal. There's average. There's stats and facts. But magic never comes from the parts of us that are average.

Each of us has our own story, our own identity, we come here perfectly. And once you believe this? It changes everything.

You're about to pull up at the great big drive-through window of life and place your order. Your life. It's a big one. Not many people know exactly what they want. There are some easy options. There are some scary ones. You could drive straight through and get someone else's order. But every action will be a choice. And if you don't ask, you won't get. You don't ask? You can't get.

We have never been in a more fantastic world; where kids get online and start million-dollar companies, where octogenarians go to college for the first time. So, when you order: be specific, be sure, and be ready! You have the potential to be, do, or have anything – and everything – you want. Why not? Better yet, *What if?*

Autism opens up a new world. A world that is more sensitive, more conscious, more aware. A world that faces complex problems with diverse brains. A world where sensitivity is power, and where energy is spent on creative solutions, not conformity. A world that needs your voice, and your shine, more than ever before.

For autistic world domination you need two things – a hero and a world. You've already sorted the hero (they're wearing your shoes), and as you work through this book you will design and dominate your dream world!

Picture it: Your life. Big time. And you call the shots. The chapters of this book are scenes, and scene by scene, step by step, they will build on each other as you script your life. This is your official welcome to the new world – welcome to autism!

Scene One: Neurodiversity Is the Key

On the outside, human brains all look pretty much the same. Pink, squishy, crinkled. But inside? The way they work? Epic diversity! We all have different brains, and we all have different strengths and challenges that come with them. Like the pins and tumblers of a complex lock, the world is full of different projects, ideas, problems, skills, talents... We need all of our different brains to unlock the magic!

In this scene, we'll create a personal vision. This vision will set the foundation for your new world.

Scene Two: World Domination

A diagnosis is not a prediction. It does not change your child, your friend, or you. It just lights up tools and strategies to thrive. You are exactly who you are supposed to be. Even when it doesn't feel like it – maybe even especially then.

Let's dig up the things that get you excited and find ways to bring them into your life. We'll define and design exactly where you want to go. And we'll dream: big, bigger, biggest, and mind-blowing!

Scene Three: Reframe and Target

Language developed to let us label, classify, sort, and categorize. And now? It's time to move from binary to spectrum. To embrace multi-layers of words and being. Change your words, change your world.

We'll get SMART and set up your targets. You will feel the deliciousness of anticipation because your perfect world is well within your sights!

Scene Four: Sensitivity Is Power

The human brain is exposed to eleven million bits of data every minute. Like canaries in a coalmine, autistics sense things sooner, and more strongly. Get ready to see how these sensitivities can make the world better for everyone.

You will figure out your challenges and dig up more of the truth about you. You'll get even braver and learn how to handle the three kinds of fear: brain, heart, and kryptonite.

Scene Five: Human Mercury

Neurodivergent brains process the world differently. Envirosynthesis. We hold on to more data, file it, feel it, deal with it, express it, process it, all in different ways. Experience the way autistics read and respond to the environment as human mercury.

This is it! We're going to take your dreams and set up a plan. We will aim for your perfect world. Aim for it and get ready to take over!

Scene Six: Energy and Fire

We have an allocation of energy. We choose how we spend it, with our words, our actions, and decisions. The energy I spent as a child trying to fit in, as a teenager trying to find my place, as an adult trying to prove myself... I could have studied physics, discovered elements, flown to the moon. You have one life. Where do you spend your energy?

As you take over your world, you will start to feel the power that you were born with. Your life is an incredible force. You can change, create, grow, inspire... it's all up to you! What are your intentions?

Scene Seven: Autism-Friendly Is Human-Friendly

Across the globe, organizations are creating sensory-friendly spaces. And the surprise? Not only do the autistics thrive, but other neurodivergents and neurotypicals engage, relax, and blossom. When we listen to the most sensitive members of our society, all people benefit.

You only have control over one person. But you are not on your own! Recruit your world domination army. Persistence, enthusiasm, desire: we'll find ways to get to the yes!

Scene Eight: The Bridge Builders

Your differences give you the ability to walk in many worlds: across cultures, across paradigms. As the world changes, these skills – translating and interpreting, balancing between realities – are as relevant and valuable as any technology or trade.

You can try to attack your weaknesses, or you can find the way they fit together to make you perfect.

Scene Nine: The New World

When there's something about you that feels weird or different, maybe even bad, remember: there are lots of other people who feel the same way. And they might not be in your family, in your classroom, in your school, or in your city, but they are in the world. You will find them, they will find you. It's time to honour your sensitivities and acknowledge your needs. Because the new world is here, and ready when you are.

Scene Ten: Autistic World Domination

Autistics feel harder, think deeper, burn brighter, and die sooner than the average. But if you are autistic, you are not broken. You do not need to be fixed. Every weakness is a strength in the right environment. And every person has a place in their culture and on this planet. Enter the magic of autistic joy!

Here, you will let go of your beautiful plans and detailed goals. You will relax, have faith, and know that you are open to the ultimate possibilities.

Scene Eleven: Sample Blueprints

And finally, some examples of how your blueprint, tailored to your own interests and goals, can look in practice.

Your existence rewrites normal. The autistic revolution is now!

Neurodiversity Is the Key

Right now, nearly 70 per cent of human beings are neurodivergent. Autistic, dyslexic, gifted, sensitive. And the number is growing steadily every single year. But this is not an epidemic, this is a revolution. A shake up of every system designed by and for neurotypicals. A total global overhaul.

> *He wā tōna ka puāwai mai te tītoki.* The tītoki tree blooms in its own time.

I stumbled out of the psychologist's office and into a different world. When I was diagnosed autistic as an adult, I was gutted. I was angry, scared, and sad. I was like most people, I didn't know a lot about autism, and what I did know was bad. Autism was *Rainman* and less-than. Autism was disabled, degrading, dependent.

But over the next few years as I adjusted to my new identity, I read and learned as much as I could. Slowly, I started to realize that all the times I had been called oversensitive, difficult, antisocial, all the times I had cried as a child, all the times I had hated myself for not being enough – I was reading and responding to my environment. I wasn't broken. I wasn't alone.

Actually? I was challenged and disabled in ways that weren't recognized. Without even the validation that acknowledging my identity would provide. And it wasn't just me. An entire generation of autistics has gone undiagnosed, and even those that were diagnosed have been dehumanized, othered, and even 'treated' to have their autism cured, fixed, or dulled.

The average life span of an autistic person is thirty-six years. Less than half that of the average population.[1] To be fair, different studies put the autistic life span anywhere between thirty-six and fifty-four, but either way, it's not one hundred, is it? Human beings are skipping around yay-for-modern-medicine-and-quality-of-life-now-people-are-living-to-over-one-hundred; meanwhile, autistics are drowning, we are being killed by our caregivers, taken out early by stress-related disease, and more than anything: we are killing ourselves.

So, many autistics don't get to grow up. We don't have elders, we don't have examples, or role models to show us the joy of perspective or time. Our history is crushed under neurotypical society, but our culture, our traditions, our resilience, are carried in our DNA. And somewhere under the conditioning, the oppression, and the colonization, we know who we are. And we know each other.

Every human, every brain, is here for the same reason: Find your calling, speak your truth, feel your way in the world. All things that come naturally to autistics. Actually? So many of the things autistics do that appear weird or different, inconvenient or problematic, are aspects of the world well overdue a rewrite. So, let's rewrite it. Let's reframe it. Let's design a world where autistics are free to be themselves, and maybe even valued for it.

The traditional diagnostic criteria for autism are deficit-based. The traits are symptoms, challenges, and difficulties, responses are behaviours. Medical professionals look for communication *issues*, social interaction *issues*, sensory *issues*. So many autistics feel broken because that is how we are seen. Described by our deficits. It's time to see our strengths. To consider the possibilities. To change the way people react when they hear about a neurodivergent diagnosis. No more sympathy. No more 'Oh, I'm so sorry'. It's time for autism awe! Curiosity and excitement! (Or at least confirmation and relief!)

Our world has complex problems and needs magical brains to find solutions. However, this is not how I reacted to my own autism diagnosis. After years and years of unknowingly masking my autistic traits to blend in to the neurotypical world, I had a breakdown. I was in my thirties and my body had stopped doing my bidding. Like a toaster with the plug pulled out, I was there, but just... gone. I went to the doctor and... honestly? I was hoping for a tumour. A clot. Hear me out. As far as I was concerned, I was broken, and I needed to be fixed. I wanted there to be a physical something that I (or ideally, a medical professional) could remove or destroy. An extra doodad, a missing piece, a loose screw.

When the doctor said 'You're autistic', I was angry. I was scared. She was confirming my worst fear and endorsing the things I had been told my whole life: that I was different. Strange. Weird. A tumour can be removed. A sickness can be healed. Autism is not some removable part of me, it is all of me. I am autistic. Truly, innately, irreversibly, autistic. It is not something I *have*; it is who I *am*. I can't remove or destroy it. And they were right.

I was diagnosed autistic as an adult, too late to change the direction of my life, but as it turned out, perfectly timed to change the way I saw it. As I read more and learned more, things became clear: Suddenly a lifetime of feeling weak and different was re-interpreted with a fresh lens: Suddenly: oversensitive was supersensitive. Suddenly: too intense was focused, and suddenly, I wasn't a broken regular person, I was a perfect autistic person.

Like animals with heightened senses, autistics live in a world that looks, sounds, and feels different. In the natural world, we celebrate diversity, some animals are fast, some are strong, some can climb really well, but can't swim. We don't question the accuracy of detector dogs or mock fish for not being able to climb trees (except of course, the three species of fish that actually can climb trees*). We watch *Animal Planet* in awe, we trust and believe that different brains interpret the world differently.

And it's the same with people. Some people can run fast, some learn fast, some can concentrate for long periods of time, some squint and see magic, or flinch at spelling errors. And all of these differences are designed to work together and make the world amazing.

Neurodiversity is a biological characteristic of human beings. The word was coined by Australian Judy Singer in 1998 and it is the understanding that humans are diverse, varied, in our brain function.

> Neurodiversity names a biological reality, the virtually infinite neuro-cognitive variability within Earth's human population. It points to the fact that every human has a unique nervous system with a unique combination of abilities and needs. That is all. – Judy Singer[2]

Neurodiversity is some people running on Linux, other people on Windows, some on Mac, others using a combination of systems, and still others programming completely new systems from scratch. We are all neurodiverse. But what about those of us with a brain that isn't typical? Autistic, hyperactive, dyslexic, with mental health issues, post-traumatic stress, epilepsy... all of us who have brains that differ in some way from what is (supposedly) the majority. Kassiane Asasumasu coined the

---

*   Examples of species of fish that can climb trees: Mangrove Killifish, Climbing Gourami, and Climbing Catfish.

words *neurodivergence* and *neurodivergent*. She says, 'neurodivergent refers to neurologically divergent from typical', and this includes innate and acquired neurodivergence.[3]

> ▶ *Innate neurodivergence*: This is neurodivergence a person is born with, such as autism, hyperactivity, dyslexia, dyscalculia, giftedness, sensitivity, and Tourette's. Indigeneity (see box) is another key innate neurodivergence.

Different ethnicities, nationalities, and cultures bring different ways of seeing and experiencing the world. Indigenous minds are often in tune with the environment, they connect and communicate in distinct and significant ways. This innate neurodivergence holds strong even through many generations of colonization.

> ▶ *Acquired neurodivergence*: Neurodivergence a person takes on from trauma, culture, long-term meditation, or mental health challenges. This neurodivergence features boosted creativity and empathy. It offers a unique way of experiencing the world. People in the Deaf and Blind communities may also identify as neurodivergent.

Neurodiversity is biological, natural, and more than that: valuable. Harnessing the skills and energy of neurodiversity is the key to innovation, to greater empathy and understanding. Understanding neurodiversity is key to the new world.

For an idea of the difference between neurotypical (neurologically typical, shortened to neurotypical or NT) and neurodivergent (neurologically divergent or varying from typical, shortened to neurodivergent or ND) brains, consider the individual's strengths and challenges. With these plotted on a graph, a neurotypical brain has a nice smooth profile, there is less of a contrast between strengths and challenges. The individual is fairly strong in some areas, such as concentrating for long periods, and fairly weak in some areas, such as calculating numbers. Meanwhile neurodivergent brains have a greater contrast between strengths and challenges. So, autistics can bring hyper-focus and attention to detail. But we tend to not waste brain space on social skills like answering 'How are you?' #SorryNotSorry.

People with dyslexia can be epic problem-solvers with a strong work ethic, but can need support with forms and fonts. Doesn't it seem kind of silly to focus on the few things people can't do, when the things they can do are so stunning?

Neurodivergent brains can be confusing to the people around them. The neurotypicals see us handling mental tasks beautifully, easily even, but then dropping the ball in the simplest social situation. To them, these skills fit along the same continuum, but to us? They are completely different worlds.

Oh, and remember to take into account people who are *twice-exceptional* (see box below) and/or *multiply divergent*.

Twice-exceptional is when a person is exceptional (outside the norms) in at least two areas. For example: an adult who has a high-IQ, and is dyslexic. Or an eight-year-old who is a voracious reader, and can't tie their shoes. A person can be exceptional, above average (e.g. with creative, motor, intellectual, perceptual, or leadership skills), while also being challenged in the current world (e.g. dyslexic, autistic, obsessive compulsive, dysgraphic, etc.). The person has superpowers, and also challenges that combine to create the kind of kryptonite that can all but eclipse their gifts. They're working really hard, but their work can't be seen.

Twice-exceptional (sometimes written as 2e) looks like an epic vocabulary but handwriting scrawl, or using all of your clever brain to figure out social navigation, so you're coming across as clever but lazy, or – even worse – average. This is how being twice-exceptional can contribute to misdiagnosis.

'She can't be autistic, she makes jokes!' – But maybe she's used her epic-memory to study social skills and memorize jokes, so she can more easily cope with neurotypical conversations?

'They can't have dyslexia, they were in the school play!' – But maybe they found an audio version of the script and memorized it? Maybe they stayed up late for weeks beforehand working on the words so they could avoid needing a script at school?

Multiply divergent (see box below) is having more than one neurodivergence at once. People can be indigenous and gifted, or have Tourette's and a brain injury. A high percentage of autistics also have exciting things going on with their attention wiring (currently known as ADD or ADHD). These combinations can make diagnosis more complicated and identity more complex, but offer incredible magic and insight in creating a new world.

Co-morbidity (from the Latin *morbus* meaning *disease*) is a medical term used when a patient has two or more co-occurring conditions. For example, autistics are known to more likely experience anxiety, depression, giftedness, Tourette's, dysgraphia, atypical sleep patterns, food allergies... But what about when you don't consider these things diseases? Some are the consequences of being neurodivergent in a neurotypical world. Others are neurodivergencies, as valid and valuable as being autistic. In this case, let's replace *co-morbid* with *multiply divergent*. Language matters, and we'll talk more about this in Scene Three.

Sameness is about survival. From a very young age we look to the people around us to define who we are. Like the dyslexics who watch other kids touching the words, they pretend to read, keep their heads down, and never get found out. We adapt, we adjust. We change who we are to be accepted and to belong. We make decisions about who we are and who we are able to be. We open possibilities and we cut them off.

There is a spectrum, a kaleidoscope, a buffet of brain candy. Kids who can argue semantics but sleep with the lights on. Adults who can run companies but are afraid of the phone. Asynchronous. There's a kaleidoscope, but the key elements are the same: sensitivities, overwhelm, and experiencing the world differently.

Autistics talk about sensory sensitivity: feeling scratched by clothing tags, burned by touch, scraped by flickering light, being kept awake by the hum of the power grid. In the same way a detection dog isn't being overdramatic and a canary that dies in a coal mine isn't being difficult, these are physical sensations.

Butterflies taste sugar 200 times[4] more strongly than humans. Different brains, different sensations, but all valuable, viable realities. When do you feel happy? (Not the Everything-Is-Perfect kind of happy, but the Just-Totally-in-the-Moment-Light-and-at-Peace kind.) When you are happy, your brain relaxes, your heart glows, and your world flows more easily. And you know what? No matter what background, brain, or meat-suit you have, you deserve to be happy. You really do. Not just because you are awesome (because you are), but because the great big drive-through window of life comes complete with as much happiness as you can order. Happiness is part of the deal!

We're here to get you exactly what you want. World domination. Why not? You have the potential to dominate your world, and experience incredible happiness, starting now! (Oh, and when you hear 'world domination', forget weapons and wars. Think: magical and emotional worlds; think: your reality. World domination isn't about entitlement, it's about responsibility.

Achieving world domination means empowering yourself to create the world you want.)

So, let's get super selfish here and just talk about you! Only you know the infinite details of your world. Only you know the trap doors, the secret rooms, only you know where the treasures are kept. Your mission is happiness over your lifetime, and you have control of that every second!

My life changed when I started asking *What if?* So instead of thinking of myself as broken and weak, too sensitive, and too much, I started asking myself: What if I'm strong? What if I'm supersensitive? What if I'm exactly how I'm supposed to be...?

On Krypton, Superman is boring, regular, normal. It's only when he gets to Earth that he's different. That he sticks out. It never really mattered that Superman could hurl big rigs, or race rockets, he was alone. And to belong, to feel normal, he put on the glasses. He got a regular job. He pushed down his super-powers until he blended, almost completely. And like Superman, over time neurodivergents develop strategies to Clark Kent our way through life: We figure out what to say and how to look and how to be. We figure out how to fit in, but to do that, sometimes we also have to cover up our Super.

Over years and years, I've trained myself to come across as normal as possible. I've figured out just how weird I can be without setting off alarms. When to act like I know what's going on, how to nod and smile, how to keep my eyes under control. I can mimic normal, but it comes at a cost. I suck it up when lights are too bright, too sudden. Sound too loud, too much, monotonous, grating, or scrapy. When things touch me, textures, food, clothing, furniture... I deal with it inside and it is exhausting. Before I was diagnosed, I didn't realize that everyone else doesn't have that. I thought, everyone was the same as me and I just wasn't handling it very well.

So many adult autistics tell the same story: a lifetime of feeling different and alien. A lifetime of making choices for everyone else, living in fear of being found out. Autism is a way of being in and processing the world. Like all neurodivergents, we navigate a world design for neurotypical brains. And that can mean we have built a life around not being ourselves. We've made choices, but guess what? We can unmake them, too.

Your brain is the ultimate accessory. *He puna o te taonga*, a fountain of treasure. People are quick to jump on new technology, use computers, phones, apps, things we learn and use to make our lives better. Meanwhile, we're walking around with the greatest technology in our skulls! Our brains may look the same, but they're all filled with different ideas, jewels, potentials, and possibilities. For some of us, these treasures are super obvious: gifts and talents that burst out, undeniable. For others, they can take some exploring, some digging. Especially in a world where traditional strengths aren't cutting it any more. And it all depends on your point of view.

New plan! You are the most important person in your world, and the only person you have all the power over. The trick? To learn as much as you can about yourself. What makes you happy, what you truly want. And I get it, maybe you don't know what you want in your world yet, that's okay. This is blank slate time. You get to decide who you are and what you want, maybe for the first time. It can start today, or next week. But know that if and when you want to find out, the tools are here for you!

Every superhero has a purpose. Whether it's stopping crime or seeking treasure, they all have a reason to leap out of bed in the morning. Now's the time to discover yours! A personal vision reflects who you are, and who you want to be.

Think about your heroes, leaders, people who have strong personal visions. Their vision gives them clarity, and this clarity gives them confidence, style, and a purpose. Why not you?

Scary? Exciting? Ask yourself... Why do we keep so many things in our lives that make us feel less than perfect? Why do we stay in places, and with people, that dull our shine? What if it is absolutely possible, that no matter how much we stuff up, suck at things, make mistakes, or feel wrong, we are here for a reason? What if getting through the crap gives us the tools we need to achieve that reason? If you knew that this is the absolute truth, would it change how you see yourself?

Deep breath.

You've got one life, one world, and one person to get a hold of. I love the story of the pirate captain and his lucky shirt (stop me if you've heard this one). Long ago, when sailing ships ruled the waves, a captain and his crew were being attacked by another pirate ship. The crew were freaking out, so the captain called to the first mate, 'Bring me my red shirt.' He put on his red shirt, and they fought off the other pirates, with only a few getting sliced and diced. Later that night, as they sat around drinking and talking (as pirates do), a new guy got brave, and asked the captain, 'What's up with your red shirt? Why do you wear it into fights?' The captain told him, 'If I'm wearing a red shirt and I get cut, the blood won't show, so you guys will think I'm cool, and keep fighting.' Smart thinking. The next morning, the lookout screamed, pirate ships were all around, loading cannons and preparing to attack. 'Bring me my red shirt!' called the captain. 'And my brown pants.'

In your world, you're the captain, the master, the head honcho, the big cheese. You are the ringleader, the director... Your job is to captain the ship of your life. Your crew are your pounding heart and shaking hands, your knotted stomach, and swirling head. And you lead the way with a plan. There are days that you'll do things because you believe in yourself, and then there are days when you'll pull out your red shirt and your brown pants.

A personal vision is a statement about your goals, dreams, and values. Businesses and organizations often call this a mission statement. It could even be your slogan! Your personal vision can start with a dream for your world – who you would be, and what you would do if there was nothing in your way (because there really is nothing in your way!). Wait, so what's a dream? A dream is the biggest and best you can imagine for your life. A dream has no limits! That's the best place to start. After that, a personal vision brings your dreams into everyday life.

And remember, Superman isn't Superman all the time, just when he needs to be. It's okay to Clark Kent your way through the day, even Wolverine retracts his claws! Just know, that Clark Kent is not who you really are. And when you need to, you can be Super You! You can put on your superhero persona, believe in yourself, rescue some cats/stand up for yourself/give a speech/fight a villain... and when it's all over, try to remember which phone box you left your pants in.

Super You is who you become when you are your very best self. By creating and writing down your own personal vision, you will have a tool to stay inspired!

Your personal vision can be as simple as Nike's slogan: *Just do it!*, or as meaty as the Declaration of Independence. Because, of course, your personal vision is just that – personal. Keep an open mind but know that your personal vision only has to be true for you. It doesn't have to look or sound a certain way. It doesn't have to impress anyone. It just has to make you feel good!

Or if the idea of a personal vision doesn't feel right to you, you could consider creating a metaphor for your life. A metaphor is when we take the elements of one thing and apply them to something else. For example, 'She has a fiery temper' (her fury may burn hot, but she isn't actually on fire!); 'Life is a rollercoaster' (life is an exciting ride, but you can do it outside of Disneyland!).

The word 'metaphor' comes from the Latin *metaphora* meaning *to transfer*. We're transferring one idea onto another. So, consider whether you've ever felt drawn to an image, symbol, or story that represents who you are or who you want to be. Here are some examples:

- You may see yourself as a racing car: powerful, motivated, and navigating through life heading for amazing prizes and checkpoints.

- Or maybe you're a sun: bright and happy, sharing light wherever you go.

- You could be a chef in the kitchen of life, mixing exotic ingredients to create delicious adventures.

- You might resonate with Odysseus, fighting monsters and temptations, heading for home.

(My metaphor is lighting fireworks – I want to spark the fuse in others! I want to inspire and motivate people to aim for the stars and dominate their world!) You can see how a metaphor can not only give you positive words to use, but it can also give you an image. You can use it to instantly feel strong, happy, and purposeful!

Blueprint Action: Your Personal Vision 🎬

Let's start by thinking about what makes you Super You. Ask yourself some questions:

> What am I good at? What do I feel strongly about?

> What do I like doing? How do I want to live?

> What makes me special? What are my passions?

> What do I want to do with my life? If you don't know, focus on how you want to feel: Happy? Excited? Peaceful?

Once you have a personal vision or a metaphor for your life, you can access your magic whenever you want. The world is at your fingertips, and your power is also your choice. For you, world domination is just the beginning. Your life is in the everyday, what you do while your plans bubble away. Love your life. Believe that it was designed for you. That every person, situation, and element around you has been hand-picked to allow you to get the most out of your time here.

And if you don't love your life? It's time to change it. Don't tolerate anything that doesn't make you glow with pride that it's yours. Love everything you eat, wear, think, and do. And if you can't love it outright, love where it'll take you. If there are things in your world that don't make you feel stoked – get them out! We're accepting way too much crap from a world where anything is possible.

Happiness is found in the everyday; it's chocolate, sunshine, puppies. Really. You can see the crap in life, or you can see the cool in life. Happiness is a choice in every moment, and you are in charge of that choice. The way to happiness is by filling your life with the things that you love. Big things – like friends, a kick-ass career, or (and!) a peaceful family life – and little things – like comfy clothes, or a jam-packed music collection.

In your life, you take all the actions, you have all the feelings, and you make all the decisions. It sounds overwhelming, but you're doing it whether you mean to or not. So, decide you're going to see it as exciting! Because that means you don't have to wait for anyone to give you permission to be happy, you can make the decision now!

There is no one on Earth exactly like you. And that's a good thing! We're here to work on your total blueprint for world domination, and it starts from a place of exquisite anticipation. Absolute belief that anything is possible – and that anything is possible for you. Know that all the achievement and money in the world can't replace a deep passion for the life you have.

We're going to get you feeling that with all your heart! Raise your expectations, and the world will meet them.

Oh, and if you're wondering about the neurodivergent majority and that statistic showing nearly 70 per cent of human beings are neurodivergent? In 2020, Dr Laura Weldon took the (US) prevalence statistics for key neurodivergencies and combined them to create a conservative prevalence estimate of 67.2 per cent.[5] This number:

- grows every year with increased awareness and diagnoses

- does not include all neurodivergencies

- assumes a likely overlap – as many people are multiply neurodivergent.

We can see that neurodivergence will continue to easily hold and increase its majority. This is the new world!

So, what's the deal? Is it that more people are neurodivergent? Is it changes to the diagnostic criteria? Greater public awareness? Dissolving stereotypes? Well, no one knows what causes autism. Scientists have ideas. But it's all theories and guesswork. All of it. It's throwing darts at mutant genes and broken brains, poor parenting, and funky diet. It's chemicals and vaccines, toxins, and mistakes. A million theories but one common theme: autism is bad.

A theory is an idea. A theory doesn't have to be what went wrong. What if we decided to go with theories and ideas that support and uplift? Okay, here's what we know:

Neurodivergents see, hear, and feel the world differently.

Everything else, every symptom, trait, behaviour, and quirk, comes from being who we are and adjusting to a neurotypical world. Everything else, every assumption, bias, prejudice, and lie, is a guess. So, let's guess. Let's theorize a best-case scenario, the little ones deserve that, and so do we! What if the cause of autism is evolution? Revolution? What if it's a breakthrough in human function? Not knowing a cause doesn't make the worst-case scenario true. You may have been gifted with a colleague, a friend, a child, or a brain that forces people to see and feel things differently, to focus on what's important. You may have been entrusted with raising the vibration of our planet.

Because what if neurodivergence delivers some of the very skills and qualities human beings need to thrive in this current world and beyond?

World Domination

There aren't spiders in milk. I say that, but everything in me knows that there are. They block the milk spout, plop into the glass, hairy, clogged with white, little black hairs flicking free. They hover faintly, just below the surface of the milk, or sink to the bottom of the glass, a prickly surprise in the dregs of the backwash.

The first time I looked around, saw people drinking milk, the spiders spinning and dissolving back into liquid, I waited for the shock, the choking, coughing disgust, or evidence that maybe their robotic insides handled the spiky arachnids with ease. Or hey! maybe even signs that spiders are delicious? Nothing.

At this point I knew two things: 1. There was no way I was ever drinking milk without the protection of heat and chocolate flavouring. And 2. No one else was like me. No one saw what I saw, felt what I felt. As long as I have been human, I have known I'm not in the same world as everyone else. On the same planet, but not in the same world. My world is extremes: sharp sounds, tangible smells, spiders in milk, and a thousand other differences in reality.

So, here's the deal: A single perfect world doesn't exist. There are billions of worlds. World domination means conquering the space around you, finding happiness in your everyday. Because there is no 'real world' – just the one you experience, the one you decide, and the one you create.

And what if that's the deal? That in some place fizzing and glowing inside us we are exactly who we are meant to be, and that our job is to figure it out, stop fighting it, and maybe even embrace it? Just stay with me for a while, and let's pretend that this is true. You are exactly who you are meant to be, and everything is happening perfectly.

Scared? Fair enough. World domination is a big deal, and it's okay to be nervous! Life can be scary. It can be stressful. You may have heard that a little bit of stress is good. Adrenalin pumping before the big game. Sweaty hands walking up to the podium. Stress can give you an edge. But it can also really hurt you. Especially long-term. Headaches, insomnia, stomach knots, and a racing brain can all be signs that it's time to look after yourself.

Biologically, we are designed to protect ourselves against threats. Our body doesn't distinguish between the threat of being chased by a viper and being confronted with the social horror of 'Tell us about yourself'. To autistic brains, threats can include sensory and social challenges, changes to expectations or routine, or any other stress. This means that when an autistic is in the world, we're basically tensing ourselves full-time, anticipating these threats. The brain releases chemicals instinctively. These chemicals will do two things:

- ▶ Deactivate bodily functions that aren't immediately important. For example: digestion. This is why when autistics are stressed, they can often go long periods without eating or using the bathroom. We'll learn more about this later.

- ▶ Engage (at least) one of the Fs:
    - ▷ Friend or Fawn: Befriending the source of danger. For example: negotiating, bribing, begging. This looks like

people-pleasing or keeping someone happy, so they won't hurt you as much.

▷ Fight: Respond with resistance. Fight physically or verbally, push or struggle.

▷ Flight: Energy and adrenalin is sent to the large muscles, ready to run or hide. The goal is to get away.

▷ Freeze: The chemical cortisol is released to numb the mind and body, like an animal that 'plays dead'. The goal is to survive and recover. The person is protected by being paralysed. Freezing is a stress-response, it is not consent.

▷ Flop: The muscles and mind become floppy and loose. This is the final defence mechanism: total submission. The goal is to reduce physical pain and protect the mind and heart.

Scanning for threats and reacting to them is unconscious. All humans do it. Autistics are just more finely tuned, so things that are ho-hum for other people can create huge anxiety for us. And when our senses become overloaded? We can experience physical reactions: meltdowns and shutdowns. A meltdown is a temporary loss of control, expressed physically. For example, crying, screaming, kicking, or yelling. A shutdown is that same breaking point and loss of control, but expressed internally. For example, going quiet, hiding, freezing, or sleeping.

Meltdowns and shutdowns are physical reactions to overload. Not deliberate, not controllable. They are breaking points. These are not go-to moves, we're not doing it to be manipulative, or because 'it works'. I don't even know that I have the words to describe how it feels to be thought of as naughty or moody, when you're already using every bit of strength to control yourself in the world.

Meltdowns and shutdowns can build up slowly, or happen all at once, parents and loved ones get really good at reading the signs. They can become experts through experience. My husband can read when I'm getting uncomfortable and overloaded – often even before me, because I am in the moment, freaking out, I don't have the presence of mind to realize what I need to do, or even that anything is wrong. Autistics can be so used to fighting our instincts, ignoring our bodies, that high-stress becomes our everyday experience. Being able to spot your own warning signs is key, and that only comes with awareness of your sensitivities and preferences, and the confidence to trust yourself.

Blueprint Action: Overwhelm

(Content warning: Stress and overwhelm.)

See if you can observe your history from the outside and give yourself some distance from the feelings. (Only do this if you can do so without re-experiencing the stress and getting hurt.) Take a moment. Can you think of times when you have felt stressed or overwhelmed? Check in with your body, what causes stress for you? Do you melt down, shut down, or both? What does that look like for you? Are there times when you react with one of the Fs? Is there an F that you use most often? Now that you know you are having a physical reaction to stress and overload, do you feel differently about yourself?

As a child I would hear things like 'She'll eat if she gets hungry enough' or 'Ignore her and she'll snap out of it'. No. To me, to an autistic child, this is not about power, this is about survival. I will starve before I will eat something that every cell in my body is saying no to. Happily.

A meltdown or shutdown is not an incident to get through or get over, it is a journey, a relationship, every day is an opportunity to build your skills, your strategies, and to get to know yourself. This is not about getting through the day – it's about supporting yourself for a happier life.

When we were children, we had little control over a world that often felt (best case) uncomfortable and (worst case) hostile. Now, as adults, it can be easy to forget that we have so much more control. We can figure out what makes us feel safe and happy, we can ask for it, and make it happen. The trick is figuring out what we need.

I had been on the same track my whole life: Push myself, isolate to recover. Push myself, isolate to recover. Time-out days from school life, weekends in bed to cope with 9 to 5 work. I didn't know it was a pattern, let alone symptoms. I thought I was weak and I was embarrassed that I couldn't handle 'real life' like 'normal people'. I was used to the up-and-down of my life, I left jobs that became overwhelming, friends that became too much. I shut down when I needed to, retreated, until I had the strength to peek back into the world.

It would have taken a lot for me to ask for help. I thought I needed to toughen up, push harder, get over it. Luckily, at that point in my life, I had children, I was working, I was coming off the back of many years of full-time work, the kind that involved huge amounts of social and creative energy. I was on borrowed time, I just didn't know it. Many autistic adults are only diagnosed when their children are (with those lists of symptoms suddenly looking all too familiar!); for others of us, it's a breakdown too big to ignore.

I lay in bed, the room lightening and darkening with passing days. I barely moved. Even blinking felt like work. Every night I would think, 'One more day…' But the days became weeks, the weeks blurred together and I lost a summer. I wasn't unhappy, I wasn't anxious, I was just… gone. Eventually I got scared. Scared enough to promise myself that when (if) I recovered I would get help.

Sometimes we don't ask for what we need, because we've never had it before. We've accepted the deal. Grown accustomed to pushing down our needs in a world that doesn't budge. We think being anxious, being stressed, being unhappy is normal.

The end of the old world starts with a safe place. A place where you can be yourself. Where you can breathe, and stamp, and cry, or sleep. A place with no expectations and no pressure. Your safe place could be your home or your workplace, it could be your bedroom or a space behind a bookshelf. It could even be inside the privacy of headphones or a journal.

Your safe space can be a physical or mental location, and you can start prioritizing time there to yourself. In whatever way works for you – gaming, reading, bathing, meditation, spending time every day on yourself.

Blueprint Action: Relax

Describe your safe place. What does it look like? Feel like? Cool and quiet, with soft lights? Warm and bubbly? Pumping music? Soft and squishy?

List three ways you can relax for a few minutes every day. Here are some ideas: nap, listen to audio books, learn meditation, learn yoga, read, write, take a walk, or watch the stars.

And know that this is not being lazy. This is honouring your needs in a world that is not designed for you. This is recharge, recovery, relaxation. This eases your racing brain. It gives you a sense of peace, and a boost to power on! You are allowing yourself to be. Not by 'doing nothing', but by acknowledging that your value is not in what you can make or do, it is in your existence. Truly.

You deserve to be here, and your presence on the planet makes you worthy.

Plus? Choosing a time and space to feel safe, to just be, gives your mind time to settle and absorb new wisdom. Your body is magical; it uses peaceful time to rejuvenate. Relaxation makes your eyes shiny, and your fingernails strong. Really! So, sit quietly, or listen to music, read, play, be with yourself. Take time to remember that this is your life, and you choose it every step. If you do this before bed, you'll sleep better. And if you do it in the morning, you'll feel happier for the day.

As a kid there were times I couldn't speak. Now they'd call it situational mutism, back then it was 'she's just shy', then it became 'must learn to speak up' on every school report, while my brain burst, and my tongue shrivelled up. Situational mutism (also known as selective mutism) is not a choice, it's not being stubborn or shy, it's a physical reaction and it takes your voice. It's also inconsistent – so you may be able to speak to family, but not at school. Speak in a group, but not when called on. Freeze on the phone but present at a conference.

This inconsistency makes it even harder to diagnose or understand. 'You're not mute, you can talk.' It's like telling people you're introverted, and they don't believe you. 'But you're so out there!' But here's the thing: You can dye blonde hair dark, you can have laser eye surgery and still push up your glasses. You can mask your differences, but you're still the same person underneath.

And that feeling of being *wrong*? It follows you. It roots down and gets comfortable. In your heart. In your cells. The more you feel different, the more you notice. Evidence mounts. The looks from people, the comments they think you can't hear. Somehow, you're always saying the wrong thing, doing the wrong thing. Somehow, there are rules that everyone knows and won't tell you. So, over time, you alter your behaviour to fit. You change your words, tweak your expressions. To fit in, to minimize the rejection. But they still notice. Parents, teachers, strangers. They give it away with their micro-expressions, changes in body language, tone of voice, word choices. Some subtle vibe, some biological instinct tells them you are different. You read and adapt to all these little signs. To survive.

Right now, you might be buried under the camouflage you have created. You might not know what makes you happy, you might not know who you are because you've been pushing it down your whole life. That's okay. This is a process.

Start with you! You are the hero of your movie. You are the captain of your ship. No one knows you better than you. If something is getting in the way of what you want, it's time to take charge! Let's jump in and figure out what makes you tick!

Life is a drive-through, a menu of limitless meals. We all have different dreams and different worlds to dominate. Your favourite food is someone else's phobia. Your dream home is someone else's worst nightmare. Your perfect world is unique to you. The universe is limitless, and your job? To identify the world you wish to dominate, your perfect world, the ultimate life *for you*. You don't have to have everything, just everything you want. And you don't have to do everything, just everything that excites you.

You can use this book to explore different ways to learn, grow, and find your edges, but maybe only some of the ways will work for you. Remember: there is no one way to get what you want. There are millions of ways! So don't use tools or resources that don't feel right, just love knowing how many options you have, and that the choice is always yours!

Maybe you hate studying books but love to talk to people. Maybe you find it hard to learn hands-on but can learn a lot from watching others. Knowing how you learn best can make your life a whole lot easier. Once you figure it out, inject it into our world. There are degrees for book-learners, apprenticeships for hands-on; there is a perfect world for everyone. You were born to discover yours! Do what feels right for you!

I wish someone had told me as a kid that so much of the world is unknown. That new things are coming through all the time. New ideas, new stories, new twists, new designs. That every day science is disproven, discovered, and that every individual has the power to send out ripples. You know, if you save seeds, you can grow endless supplies of food. The universe is abundant. There is more than enough for everyone. If you've never put yourself first, now's the time. A diagnosis is not a prediction. It does not decide who you are, what you deserve, or what is possible for you.

Figuring out what truly lights you up can help you feel excited, determined, and ambitious. You want to make the most of your time and your life! Motivation is a massive power at your command. Find yours! It's your juice, your drive! Figure out what makes you want to get up, go out, and kick ass! And be careful: I was jumping out of bed, and trucking along in an office job that was hurting me. How could I have known? I'd been uncomfortable my whole life. Sometimes I still struggle to understand what I really want, what actually feels good. But if I don't know, who does? And if I don't figure it out, who will? So, how do you dig out a buried passion? Start. Write it all down, chat with a friend, rant to yourself: you are an expert in the subject – you. To uncover your passion, start the hunt... We're about to jump into a 'brain dig'!

A brain dig is an adventure. A treasure hunt. A way to uncover your passion! First up, relax. There's no pressure. This is totally for you. Let your mind go – dream, run free – at this stage, possibilities are rampant. You have the power to design your destiny, to create your perfect world. And like in fashion, movies, and buildings, it all happens on paper first!

Blueprint Action: Brain Dig

1. Daydream! Imagine all the things you want to be, do, have, or experience. Think about how much you love chocolate, or your pet, figure out the things that fill you up, make you zing.

2. You can do this whatever way feels right for you: write in a journal, open a document, make lists, cut up magazines, take photos, go online, start a blog, make a video... Start getting an idea of how you want your world to look.

3. Find words and images that represent who you are and who you want to be.

So now, to yourself, out loud, in your head, on paper, whatever feels right, continue your brain dig, tune in on you:

4. Start hunting for things that really resonate with you, things that pull you - anything - an event, a product, a place, a colour, or word. Focus on that one thing and develop your thoughts: What does it mean to you? How could you grow it? Bring it into your life? How would your life be with more of that in it? Let's define and design exactly where you want to go. And feel free to dream big, bigger, biggest, and mind-blowing!

Remember: don't make any choices, no decisions are necessary. Don't judge your dreams, just want them! Find the things that make your heart pound and immerse yourself totally in them.

Your perfect world is powered by passion and comfort. An overwhelmingly positive feeling of joy, purpose, and belonging in your life. And if you don't have that right now? Get ready. Knowing what you don't want is powerful. It will direct you to where you want to be. And when you uncover your passion, you'll know:

- ► The thought of it fills you with energy.

- ► You feel warm and happy.

- ► It gives you a sense of purpose and drive!

What kinds of passions are there? A passion can be absolutely specific ('I want to study biodiversity in New Zealand!') or totally general ('I want to work with fluffy animals!'). For some people, it takes a lifetime of exploring and adventures to nail down their passion, and for some people it may change all the time – you may have one passion when you're ten, another when you're twenty, or a different passion every week! You may have one passion that radiates through your entire world ('Music is everything!') or feel different passions in different areas ('I love being a good sister; it's fun to spend money; purple is the best!'). The main thing is to start looking for the feeling of pure, positive, passion. Find the things that light you up. Why not fill your world with joy? Why not seek happiness wherever you can find it? You only get one shot – so live your life with whatever happiness grabs you!

And while you're looking, feel the difference between *wanting* something and *loving* it. Loving something lights you up inside, wanting it leaves you grasping. Ask yourself, why do I want it? And (especially!) how does it make me feel? For some people, their heart is their guide. For others, it's an adrenalin jolt, a brain quiver, or an irresistible pull. But however it shows up for you, it will feel like home!

Blueprint Action: Your World

It's up to you. Think: What do you want for your life? Think big. This can be as big or as focused as you decide. What do you want to be, do, and have? Look at your world from space. From here, you can see that your world can be made up of lots of different areas and explorations. Like what? Like:

Be (self-development, spiritual, beliefs, religion)

Do (education, professional, career, image)

Connection (animals, characters, family, friends, partner, other)

Have (abundance, love, money, stuff).

Once you start designing your perfect world, the universe will send you more: more signs, more jewels, more for you to add. You'll start tuning in to what you like, what feels good. Remember your perfect world is always changing, because you are always changing too! And as you define each area and imagine the different areas of your world lighting up, you can create action plans for each one.

This is the part where anything is possible! So, whatever you want in your world, include it here! Love acting? Go for the Oscar! Want more colour? Imagine the colour scheme! If it makes you feel good, it is your path. Aim high! Target joy! We're not just ordering the chance to play sports for a living... we're ordering a gold medal for swimming at the next Olympic Games. Think bigger. And biggest! And do it totally pure, that means right now don't worry about hows or why-nots, don't let yourself worry about whether you can or who-do-you-think-you-are? Bits of your heart and your brain store your future plans. This is about telling those parts of you that you expect success! And you expect it big!

Hey, right now you might not even want to think about this. Then don't! Skip this part. Only you can decide what your perfect world looks like, and no one has to know where you begin, what you include – or what you leave out. If you feel ready, go over the list. What jumps out? Is there anything in your life right now that you love? Anything that clicks for you and feels right? Or are you starting from scratch? Both are powerful. Truly. If there is an element of your life that works for you, that is comfortable and *home* for you, you can build from there. Or if you feel scared, like a stranger in your world, go with that. Starting from nothing means everything is possible.

And why do this? Because when it comes down to it, we all want the same thing – happiness. And the way to happiness is by filling your life with the things that you love.

Bonus: Look around you. Look at the things that surround you in your life now – the posters you have up, the piles of things you wake up seeing, the books you read. Look at the clothes you wear and the things you own. Touch them and feel their effect on you. *Do you love them? Do they make you feel good?*

When you're digging around in your head looking for things that give you that wicked feeling (the feeling that with that job, book, friend, or shirt, your world is complete), know that digging out what you love can mean getting dirty.

Sometimes the things that make us the happiest are the secret dreams, the art project you're scared people will judge you for, the '57 Chevy that you dreamed of as a kid. Maybe what really gets you going is dancing or numbers, painting, or texting, but figuring it out is the first step. Maybe what you're looking for is something deep, dark, and forgotten about. Something from long ago...

Like, how much of yourself did you change at school? Maybe you loved art, but you could never get the bottle looking even on both sides – so what did you do? Maybe you dropped art and picked up geography. Maybe you did it because you knew you could get higher marks with that subject, because it's a sensible choice, it would make your parents happy, help you get you a good job, stability... You may have buried yourself in a million tiny ways, changed yourself to belong, and that's why we have to get dirty here! Following your passion may not be the easy, sensible-looking path. Your true passion may be that thing you were good at when you were five but got teased about. It could be that you know what you're *supposed* to do, what you're *supposed* to be excited about and interested in... but that doesn't mean it's what you actually want to do.

As already mentioned, diagnosis is not a prediction. It does not change a child, a friend, or you. It just lights up tools and strategies to thrive. You are exactly who you are supposed to be. And once you believe this? It changes everything.

We live on the same planet, but not in the same world. And it's time to stop wasting time and energy trying to make yourself fit. Let's dig up the things that get you excited and find ways to bring them into your life.

Focusing in on your passions doesn't have to be quick and might not always be easy. But learning makes failure impossible! Because if your goal is to learn, you can make the best out of every situation. There are so many choices, so many options. And it can be incredibly frustrating if all you do is come up against subjects, projects, people, and ideas that rub you the wrong way. Luckily, you can be sure that figuring out what you don't want is just as important as knowing what you do! So, embrace and hunt down every opportunity to learn. Not just through your own experience, but by listening to people, reading books, and watching TV or movies (the experiences of others). You don't have to know everything. But every time you knock out an area of life that is so-so for you, you're another step closer. You can be just as proud of saying 'I don't want to be a nurse, a chef, or work with numbers' as saying 'I want to be a teacher'.

The most important things you'll ever learn will be about you, they will make your life smoother, easier, and more fun. Knowing yourself lets you develop your world and tweak it to fit you perfectly. Start now!

The point of this scene is to open your mind. Promise yourself that being happy matters. That from now on, you come first. Take your time, be curious. If something grabs your attention, follow it through. If it looks interesting, find out more. You don't have to be the best at everything, but you can be the best at understanding you! Don't you want to know why you get mad, or why you can't stop smiling? Don't you want to know why sometimes your heart aches, and you don't know what for?

I'm neurodivergent, it feels right to me: I want to be out. I want the label because it comes with freedom. To be who I am, and to know that anything is possible – in spite of, and because of, my wiring. I've proven that I can make things happen, but now I want to learn how to focus on what's good for me instead of what's right for the world.

And if you're here and you're neurotypical, yay for that too. I need you guys to help me navigate the neurotypical world, and to remind me that there aren't actually spiders in milk.

Reframe and Target

Right off, let's get something straight: I don't *have* autism. Autism is not something I have, it's not something I live with, or suffer from. I don't think I'm a wonderful person buried under the awfulness of autism. I'm autistic, as much as I'm left-handed or a writer. It's the way I see and experience the world. It's how I am, and who I am. (But after a lifetime of beating myself up for being me, that is already a miracle.)

I get it – autism has been pathologized, meaning everything different about autistics is deemed wrong. But here's the secret: No one knows what causes autism. Not doctors, scientists, researchers – they have guesses, theories, assumptions, but They. Don't. Know.

Let's try something. A cocoon is a magical changing room... or a slimy sack of goop, depending on how you look at it. This is reframing. A tweak, a twist, a spin – and everything changes.

The word *autism* comes from the Greek *autos* meaning isolated self. Autism is defined, diagnosed, and evaluated against neurotypical standards. Here's the traditional medical definition:

> Autism is a developmental disorder characterised by difficulties with social interaction and communication, and by restricted and repetitive behaviour.
> – Wikipedia

What if we frame the same ideas in a positive way? Now the definition looks like this:

> Autistic individuals prefer a selective social circle, intentional communication, consistent routine, and their favourite things (music, food, movies, textures, etc.).

Who decides which definition is the one we use? Which definition feels better to you? Both are technically correct. But one diminishes and one empowers.

Professor Max Planck said, 'When you change the way you look at things, the things you look at change.' Now, he meant it in a literal-facts-of-quantum-physics-kind-of-way, that photons behave differently when measured, but it also holds true for the way our beliefs affect our reality. When you change the way you look at things, the things you look at change. This begins with language. *He mana tō te kupu.* Words have power.

Your world is about what you want. As we learned in Scene Two, the world that you create can be filled with things that make you happy. You went on a brain dig and started imagining your perfect world, filled with all the things that make you feel good. Now it's time to make it real!

You've divided your perfect world into lots of different areas, and you've started finding lots of things that make you happy. Ask yourself for each area: What are all the things you want to have? Want to learn? Want to see? Want to do? You can work on them all, or one at a time. You could even pick one area a month or just leave them until you feel inspired – it's your world, your choice! You don't have to figure it all out now. Just do what feels good in this moment.

Blueprint Action: Target!

Jump in and set some goals!

You've identified the areas that are in your perfect world.

You've imagined all of the things that you want in your world.

What is the biggest you can dream for each area?

Set some goals that excite you!

There are heaps of goal-setting tools online. We're going to look at the SMART goal guidelines next, and if they work for you, use them. If they don't? Skip them! Use anything that makes the process fun and ignore anything that doesn't feel good. Your goals are your business, and they are just a kick-off point. Set your goals, and when you achieve them – set more! One minute at a time, one step at a time, one goal at a time. This is your world and it's time for you to call the shots!

When setting goals, the trick is to get super specific. Have you heard of SMART? It stands for: Specific, Measurable, Attainable, Realistic, and Time-bound. Let's take a closer look!

Specific: Being specific means paying attention to detail. This is where you define your goal exactly. To get specific, think about how your goal looks/feels/sounds/smells/tastes! For example, 'I want to be successful!' is not very specific. If this is one of your goals, ask yourself, what is 'success' for you? Is it a TV marathon with Thai food on Friday nights? Being happy in each moment? Doing work that you love? Achieving a qualification? A more specific goal would be 'I want to grow my own vegetables and eat them!' This goal outlines exactly what the person wants to do, it is specific. (More on success to come!)

Measurable: If your goal is measurable, you will know when you've achieved it. For example: 'I want to be rich!' is hard to pin down. To make a goal measurable, ask: How will I know when I've achieved that goal? So, for this example, what does being 'rich' mean to you? Is it spending time with friends? Buying a car? Having a million dollars? A more measurable goal would be 'I want to save $2000 a year into my investment account!' The person who sets this goal will be able to measure when they have achieved it.

Achievable: This means asking 'Is my goal doable?' And while anything is possible, not everything is under your control. For example, 'I want to marry my celebrity crush!' Everything is possible. But the deliciousness of a goal is being able to take action towards it. When setting your goals, focus on your actions and intentions, no one else's. Make your goals achievable, by making them yours! So, maybe instead, the goal could be 'I want to open my heart and be a loving person'.

Realistic: A goal that is realistic for one person may be much more challenging for someone else. Only you know what is realistic for you. Only you decide what is possible. Don't let anyone tell you that you can't! Here's an example: 'I'm going to read a book a week for a year and review them on my blog.' For a fast reader/writer, this goal might be perfect. For someone else, maybe not. Consider how much you're taking on. Make your goals challenging, but possible! Ask yourself: are you physically/mentally/emotionally able to achieve your goal? So maybe instead: 'I'll read a book every month for a year and review my four favourites on my blog.'

Time-bound: By adding when you are going to do something, it pulls it into reality! Add a deadline, add an end date. When you commit to a date, it will motivate action. For example, 'I am going to get fit' doesn't feel very urgent. Try instead 'I am going to train for and enter next year's Mountain to City Relay'. Can you feel how much more exciting this goal is? Being time-bound gets you fired up!

Check out your brain dig. Let's get specific. We're going to make it happen! You can have goals for every area of your world or start with just one – it's all up to you. Remember: your goals can grow with you, you can always change them. So just make them perfect for you right now. And if that means your goal right now is clearing out a doom-box a day, go for it!

Reality is built on language. Is a child picky and difficult, or selective and specific? These sound like tiny changes, and they are, but over time, language builds a person's image of who they are and what they think is possible for them. Being called 'autistic' may be the simplest label you've ever been given. If you're an adult now, you have probably been called weird, difficult, antisocial, awkward, and all kinds of heart-crushing things your whole life. You may have grown up in a family that saw you as a problem. You may have studied in schools that saw you as a troublemaker. Worked in places that saw you as difficult. You may have been excluded by friends, shunned by strangers, ignored by professionals. Whoever they are and whatever they've said, they're wrong.

As an adult, you're in charge – you can eat chips and dip for dinner, and you can decide the language you use and the way you translate it. Hop in the cocoon. Slimy sack of goop, or magical changing room?

They say: 'Autistics have difficulties with social interactions.' I say we are honest and direct. We connect in our own ways. Autistic communication is fresh, clean, and clear.

They say: 'Autistics are oversensitive.' I say there are layers to this world that are only revealed to the sensitive. Perfect example: Dunstan Baby Language. It's a theory about baby language discovered by a woman with super-sensitive hearing.

They say: 'Autistics have restricted behaviour.' I say that we use consistency and routine to find comfort in a chaotic world. And as for our repetitive behaviours? I say that when we find something we love, we stick with it! Music, movies, food, people, jobs. Oh, and our obsessive tendencies and difficulty letting go? Yeah, that looks a lot like determination and perseverance.

Diminish or empower? Who decides the language we use? The angle we take? Medicine? The media? When you change your words, you change your world. We absorb our environment, the stories around us, the people, the cultures. We put together pictures and judgements of how the world is, of how we believe we are. And this is the power of words to tell our stories and to change the way we see the world.

Person-first (or people-first) language (e.g. 'person with autism') tends to be preferred by doctors, educators, and parents. It's a way of separating the person from the condition. And that's understandable – when a condition is temporary or unwanted. And for some people, it is easier to believe that autism is an unwanted thing that's latched on to the person they love, or maybe an accessory they can take off, a purse, a hat, a choice.

History: Person-first language was defined as a response to HIV/AIDS. People advocated for more respectful language, so rather than being referred to as 'sufferers' or 'victims' of HIV/AIDS, person-first language let people take their power back – they weren't victims of an illness, they weren't defined by their diagnosis. Unfortunately, person-first language started to be used with other medical conditions that were not diseases, but ways of experiencing the world (such as Autistic and Deaf culture).

When it comes to language, it's important to respect personal choice. The way a person is referred to is that individual's choice. Every time. No questions asked. Making personal preference a priority is known as person-centred language. So, this is not about what is comfortable or preferable for anyone but you. Educate yourself, listen and learn. Language evolves all the time. Research shows that a large percentage of autistic adults prefer to be referred to as autistic. But there will always be individuals who prefer Asperger's, on the spectrum, ASD, or (shock horror!) to just be called by their name. But in the end? You decide. You figure out what works for you. And you can change your mind. Anytime.

Consider this: Are you a parent? Or a person with children? If someone referred to you this way, how would you feel?

Wait, so what's Asperger's? In 2013, Asperger* syndrome, also known as Asperger's or *high functioning* autism, was removed as an official diagnosis. This is because the traits belong on the autism spectrum, and functioning labels do not support the experience of autistic people. So don't fall for the functioning labels! Words are powerful and a label can set expectations and increase misunderstanding.

▸ How would you feel to be referred to as *low functioning*? Would it narrow possibilities or open them up?

▸ And what about if you were called *high functioning*? Would you feel comfortable asking for help?

I find it funny (and not ha-ha) when people call me 'high functioning', because it definitely doesn't feel like that when I can't get out of bed, or when I'm freaking out over sensory *everything*.

---

* Hans Asperger was the doctor after whom Asperger syndrome is named. New information suggests Asperger aided Nazi child euthanasia, so is becoming even more controversial. However, not everyone connects the origins of a word to the word's meaning for them. Be open-hearted and kind, respect personal choices.

And boy, I can't imagine how wild the autistics who are called 'low functioning' get, when they are just as capable as other people (and even more so, in many ways). Functioning labels are used to describe how well an autistic can pretend to be neurotypical. It describes your reality, not ours. What you see, not what we experience. We are all autistic, with different skills, strengths, and challenges.

Hey, you'll probably notice lots of autism organizations using ignorant, outdated, and even harmful symbols, language, and ideas. Let them. These are red flags. Shortcuts to figuring out who is worth your time and energy. Autism 'experts' who use puzzle pieces, first-person language, functioning labels, and spout autism myths are letting you know loud and clear that they don't get it. Not the people who are still learning and growing, but the people who make money by speaking over and instead of actual autistics. Save your energy, stay away.

Books and resources written before 2013 (and a few after) will refer to autism as Asperger's. People who were diagnosed as Asperger's or having Asperger syndrome may still wish to identify that way (and that's totally okay!) and many autistics refer to themselves as 'aspies' (a shortened form of Asperger's).

The word *allistic* was created to describe people who are not autistic. The word is based on the Greek word *allos* meaning *other* (in contrast to autistic and *autos* or *self*). So, you can be neurotypical and allistic and neurodivergent and allistic. The way you identify is up to you. And it's okay to learn, change, and grow.

In Aotearoa, New Zealand, an indigenous *te reo Māori* way to express autism is *takiwātanga*. It literally means 'in his/her/their own space and time'. Ooh, and isn't that exactly it? It's a spectrum, a kaleidoscope, a buffet of brain candy – and how can autism cover such a contrasting range? Some of us like tight hugs, some of us don't like to be touched, some of us communicate without words, others are super-verbal or hyperlexic – we're all so different, a spectrum, right? But what we all have in common is a very different way of being in, and experiencing, the world.

Autism is a word that comes with a great deal of prejudice, fear, and misunderstanding. It is rarely seen as a positive, and even less often actually celebrated. Now, with *takiwātanga*, there is a word that allows a solid understanding of this way of being, along with a deeply personal interpretation that can be as individualized as the autism kaleidoscope itself.

Developed by interpreter and expert Keri Opai in 2017 for the Aotearoa Health and Disability sector, *takiwātanga* is part of an online glossary of *te reo Māori* for use in the mental health, addiction, and disability sectors.*

For me, it took a long time to accept my autism diagnosis. My resistance was largely due to the language. I don't feel disordered, or 'less than' anyone else. But the *kupu*, the word *takiwātanga* lifted a weight from my shoulders. I feel that *takiwātanga* honours who and how I am as an autistic person. A word that encapsulates how I feel and the best way to be with me in a clear, concise, and empathetic way. Having *takiwātanga* as a conscious and connected way to describe autism is a gift. And distinctly New Zealand.

Imagine: You have just been diagnosed and you are full of fear and limitations, and suddenly there is language that uplifts and empowers. Imagine: Autism as *takiwātanga*, 'in his/her/

---

* www.tereohapai.nz

their own time and space'. Imagine: ADHD as *aroreretini*, 'attention goes to many things'. Doesn't it instantly change how you see things? The potential and power rising to the surface with a simple change of words?

Why can't our medical terminology be born out of awe? Out of love, kindness, or at least plain old objectivity? Why so negative? So deficit-based? A perfect example: The autism profile Pathological Demand Avoidance (PDA). Wow! Here come these brave, strong, innovative autistics, they're resisting norms, questioning the status quo, looking for depth and meaning, and we basically label them 'difficult' (if not 'impossible') before they even get a chance to shine. Imagine a new label that embraces this fierce spirit? That challenges the people around the autistic to step up, not give up?

Language evolves as we do, words that used to be everyday are now unacceptable, and words we're using now may, in time, be considered toxic, prejudiced, even abusive. And this is not about being politically correct, this is about uncovering and owning who we are, as individuals, as cultures, as precise communicators. This is about finding ways to truly see and honour each other with words.

Let's think about you, as an autistic, as an individual. How do you think of yourself? What language do you use? How have you been described by the people around you? I don't know about you, but I had plenty of labels as a child. Autistic would have been a focal point for the negativity I felt about who I was. Instead of me being the one who was antisocial, miserable, negative, difficult, it would have been the dreaded autism.

Blueprint Action: Reframing

List the negative ways you have been described. By professionals, family, strangers. I'm sorry. I know this part sucks. This is where you remember the whispered hurts, the cutting digs, and the eye rolls. This is where you hate yourself for not being able to outgrow the ways you were weak and wrong and different. You can write these words down now, and know that it was never okay. You didn't deserve this language, and the baggage and beliefs that grew from it.

Now, time for some reframing. And I'm not talking about toxic positivity or inspo-porn, not your 'special gifts' or a patronizing 'good on you for trying', we're talking about real-life, concrete, everyday strengths. You'll notice that not only are these autistic traits awesome, but sometimes even downright intimidating!

Negative traits	Reframe (Your powers!)
Obsessive	Dedicated, intense
Rigid	Consistent
Oversensitive	Highly tuned
Negative	Realistic, prepared

Imagine if you had grown up hearing the words on the right in the Blueprint Action box. Imagine if there had been someone in your life who saw you as not only okay, but as perfectly yourself. If you can't flip the words, see if the ideas below can help.

- ▶ *Honesty*. Ask an autistic a question, get an honest answer. Positive or negative, if your child, your partner, your colleague, or your friend is autistic, you can expect to hear the truth. In our mixed-up-fake-news-Photoshopped world, this kind of loyalty and truth is so valuable, if you can handle it.

A warning: For me, this is one of the hardest parts of being human. People say they want honesty, right up until they get it. Not only is the truth often super subjective, but there are also layers and layers. The truth: what we know is true and choose to ignore, what we don't realize is true but is, what we pretend is true but isn't... Autistics can communicate with a million words, or no words at all. But what they do without question is deliver truth. Autistics are known for honesty, or as neurotypicals describe it: being rude, blunt, refreshing, funny, or socially awkward. I've found when people ask you to 'tell the truth', 'be honest', or 'just say what you think' they almost always mean *make me feel better*. Just seconds after asking for the truth, people will be hurt, angry, or disappointed that you give it.

▶ *Our passions can be all-consuming.* Autistics with an interest will be more dedicated and committed to learning everything we can. So much so that we may have to be reminded to eat, drink, and take breaks!

I love to work, feel the words click in place, get things done quickly and well, but people confuse me – the more I try to explain myself, the more they misunderstand me until all my energy is going into dealing with the environment instead of working with my strengths and getting things done. I can do anything, at home, on my own. People are the hardest part of life, but you can't tell anyone that because you sound awful. (Awful but right! Arghhhh.)

▶ *Autistics feel things deeply and are attuned to the sensory environment.* We are the reason many offices, homes, and public spaces are being redesigned with natural lighting, more consideration, less overwhelm. Autistics are making the world a softer, quieter, kinder place. Autistic-friendly is human-friendly.

▶ *Integrity*. Autistics generally can't be bought. Money and status are usually not priorities for us, it's not a language we speak. We're all about the task in front of us, doing the best possible job. What good is money if we can't sleep at night?

▶ *Problem-solving*. Research shows that autistics are up to 40 per cent faster at problem-solving.[6] This is because we skip a lot of the planning and impulse control tasks to spend more mental resources on visual processing. Take that executive functioning!

▶ *We take things literally*. Autistics follow rules and instructions. (Of course, the rules have to be logical, consistent, and fair. If they're not? We will pick up on that, and deem the rules pointless. Obviously. If they're not consistent, they're not rules.)

▶ *Autistics are direct and we expect the same from others*. We say what we think, we mean what we say, and we don't go digging around for alternative meanings to your words either. Unfortunately, this can mean miscommunications when so much of what neurotypicals mean is *not* what they actually say. For example, when you say to your autistic kid 'Your clothes are all over the floor!', you might think that you're asking them to pick them up. But to an autistic, you are making a statement of fact. Yep, those clothes are on the floor. If you want us to do something, be clear: 'Could you please put the clothes on the floor in your room into the laundry before bed tonight?' Autistics are often accused of literal thinking, but I think it's more literal *listening* because we hear exactly what is said. We don't assume or guess what neurotypicals are saying, when actually, smooth neurotypical communication requires just that!

▶ *Accident and emergency*. Living in a near-constant state of high-alert makes autistics naturally better in emergency situations. We will be the calm in the storm and stay logical and focused no matter what else is going on.

▶ *We perfect patterns*. Once we know how to do something, we will do it to a strikingly high and consistent standard. Make the instructions and outcome ultra-clear, and we will thrive at repetitive tasks with attention to detail.

▶ *Mindfulness*. Sensory sensitivities put the physical world front and centre to autistics. No more expensive meditation retreats or calming medications. We live in the moment with vivid appreciation of textures, visuals, movement.

▶ *Simplicity*. Many autistics have a very specific and limited diet. Pasta, chicken nuggets, fries. Sometimes pancakes for a month. Sometimes only white rice. This makes household planning and shopping quicker and easier.

▶ *Autistics are less prejudiced*. Research says we don't judge based on physical differences, financial situation, instead focusing on actions and work.

▶ *Stimming!* Autistics don't need dangerous drugs or unhealthy habits to relax, we have in-built stress-relief systems: flapping, jumping, spinning. Cheap, portable, effective, individualized stress-relief!

▶ *Specialities and interests*. Autistics can bond over our passions and interests. It may take some time for us to find our people, but once we do, we can click into life-long relationships. (And sometimes? Our people are toys, animals, or characters in books or movies.)

▶ *Resistance to peer pressure.* We don't care about social expectations and will do what we want, wear what we want, eat what (and how!) we want. Because (if we're not masking) it doesn't matter to us what people think.

▶ *Autistics often don't see hierarchy.* We focus on what's in front of us: Your actions, not your history. Your words, not your status. The facts, not office politics or personal relationships. This quality can make us challenging (but perspective-changing!) children, students, underlings, employees, and citizens of the world.

▶ *Priorities.* Autistics show the people in our lives what really matters: being present, being happy, and letting go of what others think.

▶ *Job prospects and security.* There are companies that only hire individuals with an autism diagnosis. They recognize the strengths and value of autistic employees, and we will be seeing this with more and more companies!

▶ *Awareness.* Autistics can be efficient at spotting hazards and keeping people around us safe. This is a trait that makes us excellent parents and caregivers.

▶ *The little things.* Autistics experience senses in ways that other people don't. So, while the supermarket can be a challenge, we can also be mesmerized by raindrops, in love with a song, and can get incredible joy from endless repetition.

▶ *Loyalty.* Once autistics find a schedule or place that we like, we stay. We are fiercely loyal to people, places, and ideals. We bring high levels of consistency and dependability to the world.

► *Love and connection.* Autistics teach the people around them new ways to love and connect. Without physical contact, without words, without agenda or eyeballs.

And just like that, your weaknesses are strengths, powers even. To dominate the world, you don't need to change who you are, only how you see yourself. You can laser in, and make your strengths work for you. If you need routine? Honour that. Acknowledge your needs and be okay with who you are. A rule-following, black-and-white thinking, justice-seeking workaholic? Cool. Just make sure you schedule in some breaks.

Ooh, and something to remember? You are wired up differently. Things that neurotypical brains find easy, or no big deal, can be harder for us, because of our wiring. This doesn't mean we can't do them, or shouldn't do them, it just means that if you don't find neurotypically easy tasks easy first time, *don't beat yourself up.*

For example: Because of the way our brains are wired, we have a different sense of where our body is in space (also our senses of proprioception, kinaesthesia, vestibular processing, and interoception; see Scene Four). This can make learning to drive more difficult for our neurodivergent brain. More difficult, but not impossible.

Another key difference in our wiring? Neurodivergents are often found to have difficulties with the cognitive processes that people use to plan, remember, direct attention, prioritize, follow instructions, and manage time and resources. These are known as executive functioning skills. Executive functioning skills are, well, pretty much anything that a rich and busy person would have an assistant do: time management, scheduling, paperwork... Right down to the domestic level – cleaning, washing, food prep, housing... Wait a minute, so you're telling me our magical brains that create, innovate, connect, and explore aren't designed to clean and organize? Well, that's a real shame #sarcasm. So, if you're finding day-to-day tasks tough, it's okay. Give yourself a break. Turns out, this stuff is hard for us for a reason! (I like to think it's our brains telling us that humans have more important things to do in the world than dust, but I may be biased on this!)

Yes, analysing our language is super-sensitive, and may seem picky in a world full of big issues. But our language shapes our world and can send out immeasurable ripples. What if reframing an idea or situation opens up new possibilities? Opens hearts? Opens minds? Change your words, change your world. We deserve language that reflects the way we want to see the world, and the way we want to see ourselves.

Being diagnosed as an adult can bring with it a lot of rage and sadness. We can't control how we grew up, what we have been called, how we have been described. But we can accept it. We can forgive ourselves for continuing the hurt. We can find new language and we can practise it and we can share it now.

There is so much about the world we don't know – and that includes a whole heap about our own bodies, brains, and magic. Suddenly we understand that neurodivergents have heightened senses, superpowers, we bump into things, we jump at sounds. And what if this sensitivity extends to food? What if there's a reason our autistic brothers and sisters only eat things that are white, plastic, safe?

In the next scene we'll explore how to use our superpowers to go under the hood of this world that even science is still figuring out. We don't question the gifts of detection dogs. What if autistic gifts are keys to the new world?

Sensitivity Is Power

I remember being eight years old in the summertime, taking a big fuzzy red blanket to the hot trampoline and curling up under it for hours, mesmerized by the twirling dust particles, and the way the sunbeams pushed through the spaces between threads. Getting lost in the heat and sparkles. From the outside, this was a kid under a blanket. For hours. Not playing with dolls, not drawing or colouring. A kid under a blanket. But from the inside? I was entranced, enthralled, enraptured. I was being entertained by the multiverse. I was in autistic joy.

Often, neurotypicals describe autistics as carrying out what they call 'meaningless' rituals and activities. They don't see or experience what we do. They can't. Nikola Tesla said, 'If you want to find the secrets of the universe, think in terms of energy, frequency and vibration.' What if neurodivergent sensitivities give us access to a different world?

Your body is your constant companion. Your reminder, your meat-suit. How can it be that different tastes and allergies are true for some people and not for others? It's because your body responds perfectly to you. It's designed to want what you want, and to believe what you believe. My nana was allergic to penicillin, a miracle antibiotic, and her body rejected it. We are all special and individual, but somewhere along the way we've stopped trusting ourselves and our bodies. And we need to. Because not only does our DNA provide a blueprint with a million special secrets, but after years of listening to your thoughts, experiencing your feelings, and going on your adventures, your body knows you. Every secret, every joy. Your body has been with you since before you were born, and, until we sort A.I., it will probably be with you for the rest of your life. (Personally, I'm hanging out to be a brain in a jar.)

Research tells us that eleven million bits of data come in through your senses to be filtered and processed by your brain every minute.[7] And that whole 'humans have five senses' thing we learned at school? Turns out they were just trying to keep it simple. We teach kids about the five senses, make passing reference to an elusive sixth sense, but quickly move on to teaching and learning 'more important' things. Somehow, we decided that it's more important for humans to learn mental gymnastics, to calculate, schedule, and compute, more important to know about things outside of us, than to understand our own bodies. We'll jump deeper into this later, but for now here are some examples of human senses:

Tactile (sensing touch)

Auditory/hearing

Visual/sight

Taste

Smell

Proprioception/kinaesthesia (sensing body position, grip, and movement)

Vestibular processing (sensing balance and posture)

Interoception (sensing signals inside your body)

Thermoception (sensing heat)

Emotion (sensing the feelings around you)

Alexithymia (identifying and expressing the feelings inside you).

Awesome, right? And this isn't even all of them! Neurodivergents are waking people up to the magic and power of our human senses, by showing us what happens when our bodies and minds intersect to colour our experiences of the world.

When you're autistic, senses can be either hypo or hyper – meaning our brains are processing each sense either lightly or intensely. We can be:

- ► *Sensory-seeking*. This is hypo-sensitive, meaning we feel it less so seek it out. This looks like people wanting tight hugs, strong smells, silky/gritty feelings, etc.

- ► *Sensory-avoiding*. This is hyper-sensitive, meaning we feel it more so avoid it. This looks like people with their hands on their ears to block sound, squinting when the lights are too bright, hating scratchy tags, avoiding touch, etc.

And this is why one person who loves to be squeezed tightly, and another person who doesn't want to be touched at all, can both be autistic. And depending on the sense and the situation? An autistic can be both hypo *and* hyper. Autism is a way of being in the world. There's not one spectrum, there are spectrums: no words at one end, hyperlexic (super-verbal) at the other. Office job at one end, can't leave the house at the other. And a million variations in between. This is not binary. This is kaleidoscopic.

Blueprint Action: Your Senses

What is your experience of the different senses? Have you ever wondered if you feel some things more intensely (or less intensely) than other people seem to? For each sense, are you sensory-seeking (hypo-sensitive) or sensory-avoiding (hyper-sensitive)? Does knowing this change the way you see how you experienced life as a child? How about now?

When you tell an autistic kid 'It's not that loud, it's not that bad' or 'No one else is upset by it', you tell them that their experience of the world isn't real. This is gaslighting* and it's not okay.

Many autistic adults grew up being told 'It's not that bad' or 'No one else can hear it'. We were invalidated so often that doubting ourselves became our default. This is one reason so many autistic adults have trouble articulating their needs or being confident to ask for support, because we are so used to pretending the things that hurt us don't. Now, we have to relearn to understand our bodies, to trust our senses, and to get what we need to make the world our own.

Until my adult diagnosis, I didn't know I was wired differently. I just believed I was weak and broken. For me, there is no debate around 'Shall we tell our child about their diagnosis?', 'Oh, but we don't want them to know they're different.' They know they're different, we all do. We know it, we feel it, and it hurts us. Because what we don't know is why we are different, and that our difference makes us perfect.

---

* The term 'gaslighting' is taken from the 1944 movie *Gaslight* (directed by George Cukar). In the movie, the husband poisons his wife with leaking gas. When she says she smells gas, he tells her that because *he* doesn't smell gas, she must be wrong.

One of the first autistics I met in real life was a ten-year-old girl. She is just beautiful. Beautiful, autistic, and communicates without words. She lights up the room. She radiates peace and joy. Sure, if she was a 40-year-old dude who turned his back on the rat-race to take up meditation we'd say, 'He's made it. He's there, where we all want to be. No sense of rush, of busyness, no constantly reaching, toxic ambition. Just totally present. In love with the details of life – not the ticking boxes or building bank accounts, but the dance of swirling leaves, the joy in the subtle, silent things.'

But *taihoa**– she's ten years old, so we're beside ourselves: 'She needs to get busy, get a job, she needs to contribute, be productive, be employable.'

We live in a world with higher anxiety and depression rates than ever before. We've got stressed-out-execs paying big bucks for meditation retreats, medication, recreation, desperate for work–life balance, to find ways to wind down, detox. Sit with an autistic. We'll get you there in two minutes.

We have got to stop using the challenges of autism as an excuse to deny that these strengths are intimidating: people who won't lie to impress you or to manipulate you, people who can't be bought or pressured, people who are happy exactly where they are.

But it's easy for the kids, right? The ones who are diagnosed early, the ones who grow up surrounded by 'How can we help?' and 'What can we do for you?' The autistics who come into their identity as smoothly as they come into their physical body. Casual, matter-of-fact, part of the deal. Those of us diagnosed late often come kicking and screaming. Diagnosed via break-down, burnout, bombshell. The new generations are coming through with supports, adjustments, a world already tempered

---

* A *te reo Māori* word that means *wait* or *hold on*.

to serve the sensory sensitivities some of us have fought and pushed down our whole lives.

I guess we can grizzle about how rough we've had it, how unfair it is, and we'd be totally justified. It sucks that the diagnosis, the strategies, the help that would have changed our lives as kids is now readily available. To kids. It sucks that, now as adults, we still have to fight for diagnosis, identity, support. And it sucks that we've wasted so much time believing that we were the problem. But you know what would suck worse? Wasting even one second more. On regret, anger, or fear.

What if the one thing that you're on this planet to do is the one thing you won't try? Fear can eat at your oomph. It can get in the way of the things you want, and it can suck away your power. I read that if you're not afraid, it's not brave. So, the idea here is not to stop feeling fear, because you won't win that bet. We're not going to zap away your fear – everyone has it. Fear can show you what you don't want, fear can help you decide, and fear can guide you when nothing else can. So, let's find a way to make fear work for you. Because if there's one thing we need to dominate our world, it's oomph – and plenty of it!

Now, like you did with your world and your powers, the first thing to do here is to define your fears. Get right up close and scary. What makes your skin crawl? Your guts churn? Is it spiders? Paper cuts? Public speaking?

(During this scene, watch out for your brain trying to trick you... It might be doing it already, saying, 'I'm not scared. I'm not afraid of anything!' So instead, your brain might use different words, maybe *hate*? It can seem easier to hate or to be angry than to be vulnerable or afraid. And if that makes you feel better, cool. But if you want to do something about it then let's trick your brain right back! Call this section 'Hate' not 'Fear' because life isn't about being right, it's about finding your way and feeling good while you do it!)

Let's check out the different kinds of fear: brain fear, heart fear, and kryptonite.

- ▸ *Brain fear*. Fear and hate can be things that our brain creates. We have a bad experience: a spider jumps out, a teacher embarrasses us, we nearly drown, or we eat too much cotton candy. Our brain takes that one experience and blows it up, makes it huge. Suddenly we are scared of all spiders, we hate doing maths, or we won't go near the water (or the circus). A brain fear can be something light that you are happy to play with on your own terms, like a fear of trying new food, or something common that you can easily consider logically in your mind, like a fear of heights. We can take on our brain fears – because we are in charge of the brain that creates them!

- ▸ *Heart fear*. But what if the fear is in our heart? What if we are afraid of a person or a situation? What if we fear for our life? A heart fear is a strong, yucky feeling, a heaviness, an instinct. The feeling that says 'I can't trust this person' or 'This choice doesn't feel good to me'. For example, toxic relationships or breaking the law. A heart fear is dark, heavy. It might feel like shame or even your conscience, a warning. Because sometimes fear lets you know that you're on the wrong path. It's a sign that says 'Go a different way' or 'This isn't safe for you'. Sometimes, freeing yourself from fear means moving away from something. From a person, a place, or a situation. When your heart feels fear, you are allowed to run. You should run. Trust yourself. Get help and support. Everyone deserves to feel safe in their world, especially you. With a brain fear, you feel strong when you say yes, or push through. With a heart fear you feel strong when you say no, or walk away.

► *Kryptonite.* What if your biggest challenge in life is something you can't change? Something about your brain, your body, or your family that's out of your control? Like Superman, even with all his superhuman strength, one lick of the element kryptonite, and Superman's powers are gone. Luckily, Superman knows this. He's figured out that he probably shouldn't hang out in kryptonite malls or wear kryptonite pyjamas. But imagine if Superman didn't know about his kryptonite issue... he could be out shopping and not know what hit him. Same for you; you have your powers, but you have your challenges, too. The trick is to know what they are without letting them consume you.

Brain fears, heart fears, and kryptonite. Now that we know the difference, let's get to you! Begin with brain fear. Start thinking about how different brain fears might affect your life: Are you afraid of being alone? Afraid of failure? Afraid of having no money? Are you worried about what people think of you? No one else needs to know, so be honest here.

Blueprint Action: Fears/Hates

1. List the fears/hates you have for each part of your world.

2. Look at your list carefully.

3. Decide whether you want to tackle any of them (you don't have to!).

Look at your list. Make a decision. Are these things bigger than you are? No way. Will they get in the way of what you want?

Maybe. Do you have to overcome them all? No, not all of them. Sometimes courage looks like walking away. *He toa taumata rau.* Bravery has many resting places. Some fears you'll need to attack full on, some you'll decide to let yourself have, and some you'll try to work on over time.

Kryptonite can be a secret strength. Don't be afraid of not being perfect, it might be what makes you amazing.

You can choose to tackle or ignore any part of your life... if you are willing to accept the consequences. One thing I can tell you – there is an incredible power that comes from taking on a challenge. From knowing that you can overcome something that seems to be ready to crush you.

After high school I fell in love. Quentin Tarantino's work filled me with more passion than my existing plan for a career in advertising, so I left to study film. When the course was complete, my passion was all but dead. I had gone to film school expecting to feel a sense of unity. I had expected to meet people that loved movies like I did, people who wanted to change the world through storytelling. Instead, lunchtime conversations were filled with 'How much directors earn' and 'Quentin who?' My classmates were confident, bold, and full of sass. I shrank into the background. I didn't belong there. I knew it, and so did everyone else. Film school was my first big heartbreak. It hurt like hell that something I wanted so much could feel so wrong. And on top of knowing that film was wrong for me, I suddenly felt like I couldn't go back to my old life either. There was no Plan B.

I wonder now if it was bad timing, my perception of the other students, or part of something bigger... because my dreams, my blueprint, my entire life was reshaped after that. I came home from film school and broke down. With my future dissolving ahead of me, I decided to change everything until something felt right. I pierced my eyebrow, bleached my hair and dyed it blue (before it was cool, guys), and enrolled in a

Toastmasters training course called Speechcraft. Toastmasters is an international organization that offers training in public speaking and courses designed to build confidence. I decided that this would be the perfect antidote to my post-film-school depression. I'd get a much-needed boost and add to my resume while I made a new plan.

The Speechcraft course started at 7am. Public speaking before the sun came up? Perfect. It meant people were half-awake and hopefully wouldn't remember if I was terrible. Not that I thought I would be. I planned on going in there, having some fun, and coming out with an oomph injection and a certificate.

One of the first exercises was to speak for one minute on a subject with no preparation. As soon as I was given my topic, I was super-confident: 'All the World's a Stage'. My brain kicked into gear, telling me 'It's an easy topic, I've got lots of ideas. I'm going to kick ass!' I stood up, big grin, confident. I turned to face my audience of eight. My brain speeded up, panicky. *I was sure it seemed like a lot less people when I was sitting down. Oh my god. Omigodomigod! Eyes. Just so many eyes. Eight heads, two eyes each. That's sixteen eyes, right? All looking at me, waiting for me, filled with expectations. And who did I think I was to say anything? To expect these eight grown up people to be interested in anything I had to say?* I opened my mouth and all that came out was 'Oh my god oh my god'. Screws weren't just loose in my head, the whole conveyer belt had come undone. I started apologizing. My mind was spinning and all I could get out for the entire minute was 'I'm sorry I'm sorry I'm sorry' punctuated by 'Oh my God' over and over again.

The rest of the meeting was a blur. I was panicking – what happened? Why wouldn't my thoughts sit still and come out one at a time? Why couldn't I control my own brain? But it didn't matter and I didn't care, because I was never going back. I would find some other way to get over film school, because I'd never get there by torturing myself.

Was I freaking out? Definitely. But I didn't really feel fear until the meeting ended. Because at the end of the meeting several people in this group of strangers felt compelled to approach me. Most of them told me 'It'll be all right', some of them hugged me, but all of them left me with the impression that I was much, much worse than I had thought.

I left the meeting, called my mum to pick me up, then sat in the phone box and cried. I'd gone along for some fun and all I found was another thing I sucked at. I cried. I was lost. I hated school, so I left (So boring! So frustrating!), film school was depressing (Where was the passion? Where were my people?), and now here was another thing that didn't feel right. Why was everything so hard for me? Why wasn't I normal? That's when it hit me: I didn't want there to be anything else I couldn't do. I knew I had books and movies to write, and I knew that if I wanted to do big things in this world, I would need to be able to speak. (Note: This isn't true, but I didn't know that then.) I would go back to Toastmasters, whatever it took, as long as it took, and make it work.

I was underaged when I joined Toastmasters. It's R18, who knew? No one expected a kid to want to join. No one asked. I didn't tell. And I went every week, and every week, I would hope for a car accident on my way. Not a huge one, just enough for a quick check in at the hospital and back to my day, public-speaking free. I never got the accident. But I did get better. I still feel completely sick before I speak, but the texture of the feeling is more like excitement than dread now.

My autistic traits, my obsessive tendencies, and difficulty letting go (aka determination and perseverance) is how I kept going back to Toastmasters, week after week, year after year. I had decided to keep going until I could speak. So, I did. For me at that point, success meant fighting my weaknesses, overcoming them. Pushing out, hacking away at everything I considered wrong with me.

I didn't care what it took – I've done it my whole life; from kindergarten to parenthood, I've fought hard to fit in places that didn't fit me. I have believed that if I worked hard enough, if I changed, if I figured out the ways that I was broken and fixed myself, I would fit. Autistics will keep our word, solve the problem, find the error, make things better. Because we can't not.

I was a Toastmaster for ten years (officially, although in my heart I'm a Toastmaster for ever), and achieved a lot during that time. But nothing I did taught me more than the fear I felt at that first meeting and knowing that I choose. I choose what scares me. I choose what I can and can't do. I can decide exactly how I want to handle my fears.

They teach us at Toastmasters that fear is a physical response, and your body can't keep it up for ever. I've been scared of whales for a long time (yes, I know how weird that sounds), and now sometimes I'll get a kind of bizarre death-defying thrill out of watching whale documentaries and noticing how my heart pounds and my hands sweat. Because I know that my body can't keep it up, so little by little I'm building up my 'whale resistance', and one day I'll be able to look at them without thinking I'm going to die. (Yes, I know technically they can't swallow me. My literal brain doesn't help here.) I can come up with ways to overcome my fears.

Blueprint Action: Brain Fear

Next up? Start creating strategies! What kinds of strategies? Whatever works for you! Maybe you will full-on face your fears. For example:

Scared of spiders? Get a pet one!*

Scared of public speaking? Join Toastmasters.

Hate maths? Join the Mathletes.

When you make your fear something that you do deliberately and regularly, you dissolve its power over you.

*Or (less extreme but just as effective), find the biggest, creepiest, hairiest spider picture you can. Post it up somewhere you can see it, with a note on it, *I Choose*, and smile at the picture every day.

If full-on is a little fast for you, try it bit by bit. Study yourself and notice what happens to you physically when you are afraid. What thoughts race through your mind? No one knows you better than you. See if you can change your thoughts. (Why not? They're your thoughts to change!) For example:

> Afraid of rejection? Start seeing every 'no' as one step closer to the 'yes'.

> Afraid of failure? Decide that if your goal is to try, you'll always win!

> Hate not fitting in? Know that you are special because you don't fit in!

Find ways to make your thoughts work for you.

When the fear is in our brain we can go after it, train it, and control it to change our world. But what about when the fear is in our heart? When fear is making you do things that don't feel right, or say yes when your heart says no, find someone to talk to. Go to a therapist, a librarian, or a stranger at a bus stop. Send an anonymous email. The important thing here isn't the person's job title or position. It's finding someone who gets it. Keep going until someone hears you. Sometimes walking away from an unhealthy situation can be just as hard, and just as strong, as facing a fear. Get the support you need to keep yourself safe.

Kryptonite is totally out of Superman's control. It's not something he can 'work on', he can't just 'get hard' or 'snap out of it'. Kryptonite is part of Superman's life, and his best option is to accept it, and figure out strategies to keep interference to a minimum. There are things in your world that, no matter how much you dislike them, are here to stay. No amount of planning will 'fix' your diabetes, your short-sightedness, or your dyslexia. The key is to accept these things as part of your world and look for ways to integrate them. And guess what? There may even be ways to turn them into strengths! What's your kryptonite?

Blueprint Action: Kryptonite

1. What are the things in your life that challenge you?

2. Write them down, then look at the list.

3. Can any of them be changed?

4. Understand that some challenges need to be attacked, and some need to be accepted.

5. Figure out which are which!

6. Your kryptonite is part of who you are. Can you find ways to make your kryptonite work for you?

For example: Hyper focus and super-sensitivity are awesome traits in my work-from-home writing job, not so great in an office job where I'm the weird girl who cries under her desk and freaks out when people touch her

---

stuff. It's all about finding ways to make your challenges work for you.

If you want to make a massive change and take on your kryptonite, get professional support. If you want to ease your diabetes, speak with your doctor, or if you're considering laser eye surgery, talk to an optometrist. Just because you're doing it for you doesn't mean you have to do it alone!

We are all surrounded by input, data. Images-sounds-emotions-words-textures, remember? Eleven million bits of data every minute. This is music, anger, memory, love, numbers, bugs, fizz, and sparkle. All the things that make life delicious, painful, amazing. All the details that make life, life.

So, what do we do with all this information? Our brains are powerful multi-core processors, running on multiple operating systems, they are unfathomable sifters, and selectors. Our brains filter this information inundation into bite-sized, digestible, processible chunks. This means that with zero conscious input, our brains can filter out background information, unnecessary facts, irrelevant and squirrelly detail.

- ▸ Regular brains don't hear the person next to them at the same level as the chatty mums on the other side of the room. Autistic brains often hear both.

- ▸ Regular brains don't get side-tracked with numbers, distracted by clicking insects, or overwhelmed by the smell of the three perfumes in the room. Autistic brains often don't get to decide which environmental details come in, they all come in. So, we get overwhelmed, with physical consequences.

Thanks to beautiful regular brains, efficient filters, the eleven million pieces of data coming in through all the senses are filtered and processed, down into the fifty bits per second that we can actually use. The rest barely registers.

Autistic joy can fizz with this intensity. Autistics describe being absorbed in an attention tunnel, an activity that they love. So absorbed that they lose time, they forget to eat or drink, they work passionately through toilet breaks and mealtimes (dream employees though, am I right?).

Different people have different filters, based on their brain, their experiences, their intentions, and their capacity. So, this is why if your first car was a shiny yellow Mini, you will always notice a shiny yellow Mini. Other people will just see traffic.

Regular brains filter out the unnecessary. Regular brains are ideal for focusing and for survival. But we're past survival. This is the next level.

Autistic brains, neurodivergent brains, process the world differently. Our brains take in everything. They hold on to more data, file it, feel it, deal with it, express it, process it, in different ways. We see patterns, errors jump out, subtle signs blend for conclusions, and ideas that can seem inspired but are actually right there. When you have access to more of the data (see also The Cassandra Complex in the next scene). Here's the deal:

- ▸ Plants process light.

- ▸ People process food, water, and elements of the environment.

- ▸ Autistics process everything.

This kind of enviro-synthesis is how we process the world. And right now, the world is built for neurotypical brains. And neurotypical brains don't feel the pea under the mattress, they are numb to the rising volume of life and protected from unnecessary detail, like the frog oblivious to the water starting to boil all around.

It took a long time for me to decide to come out and tell

people about my diagnosis. To go public. When I gave my TEDx talk, it was one of the first few times I had even said it out loud. Since then, I have seen a lot of change and growth in the autism space, but I still see it, hear it, feel it – the negativity, the misinformation, the myths and straight up lies. People's worlds crashing down when they, or someone they love, are diagnosed. That shame I felt, that need to keep pretending I was normal, is why I knew I had to go public. Because yes, I come across fairly normal, thanks to years and years of fighting hard to fit into the right boxes and make myself okay in the regular world. And yes, I could stay quiet, I'm an adult so the diagnosis makes little difference to my actual life.

But what if I can add another voice to this conversation? Another point of view, another example of what autism can look like? What if I could change the way a person is looked at or talked about when the people around them find out they're autistic? Spoiler alert: Autistics, no matter our age, gender, or communication style, we all know when people are talking about us, when you are being mean, being secretive, when we are problems or burdens to you. We don't have to be making eye contact to know that you respect us or don't, like us or don't.

After I spilled my guts on the magical TEDx dot, people kept calling me brave, and it's hard not to flinch at that. Going public with who I am: *tangata whaitakiwātanga*, an autistic person. I never felt brave. It felt like telling the truth.

My whole life I've pretended to be normal to survive the million things that confuse, hurt, itch, and infuriate me. But doesn't everyone do that in some way? You change your language depending on who you're with, post the pretty pictures, and skip the cold realities. We let people see what we want them to see. We determine our brand, and we maintain it.

My comfort zone is at home, in the dark, writing. Meaning I live most of my life outside my comfort zone. (Why bungy jump when you can go to a social event, right? All the heart-pounding, adrenalin-pumping fear of death without the helmet or knee pads.) Being open about who I am dissolves my comfort zone even further, but guess what I've been getting in return? A new kind of peace. A new kind of freedom. Connection with people from all over the world who send me messages of how my story speaks to them.

Your reach can be global, the rules are gone, and everything is possible. Speak up. Because it's not that we don't have challenges, fears, losses; it's that we don't share them. We worry people will see us as weak or less-than. That we will damage our brand. But authenticity is knowing who you are and creating your life around that truth. What's your brand? What do you let people see? How do you label yourself?

There is no normal, because we're all a mix of ingredients: strengths and challenges, sensitivities and specialities. A label can be empowering or restrictive, but either way it's only a part of who you are. So, put it out there – make it normal. Neurodivergent, determined, omnivore, Minecrafter, sensitive, sad-sometimes-and-okay-with-it, aspiring billionaire, ever-changing, broken, hopeful. Build on your strengths, acknowledge your challenges.

Consider what you keep hidden. And why. A re-brand is brave. You risk losing your comfort zone, you risk losing what you know. But when you open up, you connect. You share your journey, and you find your people. You carve out possibilities with people who support you. What if everything you dream of comes from being exactly who you are?

Telling the truth: this shouldn't be brave. But it is. Vulnerability, owning your stuff, opening up, and being comfortable in the uncomfortable. This is how we change ourselves, this is how we change the world.

Everyone fears or dislikes things, everyone has challenges. But not everyone faces them. You could go your whole life and never speak your truth, stand up for yourself, or hold a spider.

Or you could be a superhero, someone who goes out and kicks ass. Someone who does it in spite of their fear. You know what? Some of the bravest people I know do it with their brown pants on. You have already survived a world designed to squash you. You have made it this far and that is huge. If you're not afraid, it's not brave. Be honest about your challenges and know that you can choose. Prepare, be brave, and expose yourself! The greatest superpower is knowing yourself, and using your energy to create the world you want. Now's the time: Be brave. Be who you are. Rewrite normal.

Human Mercury

So, there I was, walking onstage at TEDx. About to share my diagnosis, about to share my story. And there it was, right in front of me: the big red dot. The most magical place to spill your guts. A place with the potential to reach the world, or at the very least to honour your truth. I remember stepping up, the lights so bright that I couldn't see the audience. I hadn't slept in a long time, I was scared, I was sick, but I was ready...

In a hospital emergency room, triaging is the process of sorting issues (usually injuries) into priorities. The most urgent issues first, the least urgent issues last. Chest pains? Severed artery? Top priority. Papercut? Standing by. This is exactly what happens physically to autistics: we triage. Just like the stress response, our brain directs resources to where they're most needed. So, if we are anxious, we might not eat. And if we are excited, we might not need sleep.

The human brain is powerful. It can override your physical instincts. Have you ever:

- ► ignored hunger pangs?
- ► held back tears?
- ► pretended you weren't in pain?

When your physical body is in trouble, your brain triages so that physical resources (oxygen, blood, energy) are sent to where they're absolutely needed. Your arms and legs might go numb because blood is redirected to your pounding heart or a bullet wound. You might go into shock and not feel pain until you're in a safe place. Adrenalin is supposed to be a survival mechanism, a short-term boost. A stress response: fight, flight, freeze, friend/ fawn, or flop. But for autistics, anxiety often keeps our bodies in the stress response as a way of coping with the everyday.

Autistics sense, spend, and breathe energy in a different way. An autistic reads the environment (emotion, details, light, chemicals) and responds as a kind of human mercury. We have an individualized hierarchy of needs, triaged based on our own strengths and sensitivities to survive a physical system flooded with cortisol and adrenalin.

Theories of human motivation give us a peek at how this works. Basic needs such as food and safety at the bottom of a pyramid, up through to love and self-actualization. The needs that are lower on the pyramid tend to relate to physical human comfort, the needs that are higher on the pyramid relate to achieving human potential. The idea is that humans must secure our low-level needs before we can move up to higher levels. For example, it's hard to finish a spreadsheet when you reeeaally need to go to the bathroom. The same way it can be harder to concentrate and learn under a flickering light.

The first priority for non-autistic people is usually physio-logical needs: food, water, breath, sleep. But for an autistic, the first priority is more likely to be safety: avoiding or adjusting to situations that trigger a stress response. Or belonging, making sure we blend in to our environment, so we aren't targeted for being different.

And safety, for an autistic, can mean quiet, low stimulation, selected people, clothing that doesn't scratch or tickle, food that is consistent. For example, for an autistic with strong sensitivity to taste or smell, or very selective eating or sensory needs, something as necessary and everyday as food can feel unsafe. Such as eating in a group environment ('What are you eating?' 'Why are you doing that with your food?' 'Is that your lunch?'). Lots of autistics don't eat at school or in unfamiliar environments. It can be seen as being picky or difficult, when actually the physical act of chewing, swallowing, and processing food while also translating social cues, and dealing with an onslaught of other sensory information with pumping adrenalin and keeping a straight face, a neurotypical mask on, is exhausting. And so yeah, sometimes that means we stick with the same food. Plain, processed food. Food that is consistent and safe. To decrease the input, conserve energy.

Until now, you've been the outsider. The world has told you that it's you who are wrong, you who are different. So, you've tried to fit in, you've changed yourself. But guess what? You are one of many. You are not wrong or different, and you deserve to live in the perfect world for you. In this scene, we'll bring your dreams into reality.

Blueprint Action: Triaging 1

What are your personal needs? Safety? Belonging? Do you have strong sensory preferences? Can you delay physical needs until these are met? Think about your life. Have you ever been so distracted by a feeling that you couldn't focus? How do you triage your needs?

When (and if!) you feel ready, jump into the next part of the blueprint. This is where we set you up with the ultimate to-do list. The path that once complete will launch you step-by-step into your new world. Head into this section with a bubbling determination! This is your path to world domination, the perfect world for you! Anything you want can be achieved, and you have the power to make it happen. Take a deep breath, the beginning is a dizzying place to be!

You've started digging for the things that make life worth living for you. Check out your brain dig. You've uncovered your passions, set your sights on specific areas, and decided to take over the world, now what?

Blueprint Action: Triaging 2

Remember, a total blueprint is no good if it dominates the wrong world! So, only complete this part if your brain dig from Scene Two makes your heart pound, and your targets from Scene Three make your feet tingle to go out and just start! That's the importance of identifying and targeting exactly what you want.

Take what you've learned from your brain dig, and picture yourself in your perfect world. Imagine yourself exactly where you want to be – and I mean big, as big as it gets. This is the day you achieve your goal. The moment that the dream is your reality. Think: Joy, Peace, Oscar, Gold Medal, Completed Certificate, Moving in to Your Home, Bedroom Makeover, One Hundred Million Dollars... (And if you're not sure where you want to be? Reread your personal vision, go on another brain dig, and have fun exploring your passions!)

The trouble with thinking big is that it starts to look hazy. Unrealistic. Mythological. So, this part of the blueprint brings it into focus. When I think about writing a book or a script that changes the world for someone else, I get that heart pounding, big-eyed, puppy-spirit feeling. If you love movies, then maybe to you the coolest, most exciting thing that represents success would be a gold popcorn for best movie, a movie award. 'I want a movie award!'

Whoa – roadblock! Who am I to think I can get a movie award? Or a gold medal? Or to even think about the thing that important/special/lucky/beautiful people do? Newsflash: You are Walt Disney before he met the mouse. You are Oprah before the talk show, Jamie Oliver before food. But better than all of that, you are you! You are the only one of you that exists, and you are on the brink of becoming who you were always meant to be. You are one decision away. Don't let that whiny little voice in your head fill you with crap that'll stop you swooping down the bat pole and making a difference! You are already exactly where you need to be, and everything you dream of is waiting for you to go out and grab it! This is your world, and you are the star. In this moment, no one is watching, and in this moment your dreams are yours. Doubting yourself is no longer an option. Don't if or but, just dream.

There's a part of you, way inside, that never changes. It just waits to be more of itself. And that little shiny glow believes in you and tingles when you start thinking about how you want your world to be. That's the part we're talking to here. Block out the bad and snuggle up to the glow. And when you're there, get cosy. Yes! You want an Academy Award, a Nobel Prize, and your own business. Yes! You want a gold medal, a scholarship, and true love. Yes! You want to aim high, live your dreams, and dominate your world. Yes! Yes! Yes! (And hey, remember these are just examples. Success is subjective and deeply personal, you decide what's best for you. Is it learning a new skill? Is it cooking a meal from scratch? Is it starting a course, reading a book, making a friend? Make your goals big enough to feel exciting, and close enough to feel doable. Not everyone wants to own a house or get a pet. Not everyone wants to get married or cure eczema. And yay for that! Find what lights you up, what feels achievable, believable, fun, and real *right now*. Make goals that matter to you.)

Okay, so now what? Kick your imagination into gear. Picture yourself in the future that's waiting for you. They're putting the medal around your neck, you're cashing the cheque or holding the diploma, you're decluttering the final box, finishing your last assignment, you're walking into your first day on the job, you're accepting your golden statue. Now think, what was the very last thing you had to do to be in that moment?... To get an award, you have to be nominated.

Play it again. So, you've been nominated. Imagine the feeling of being nominated (or qualifying for the Olympics, or completing the final paper, or dropping the last bag of donation clothing to goodwill, etc.). Think, what was the very last thing you had to do to be in that moment?... To be nominated for a movie award, you have to have made a movie.

And what would you have to do to be there?... To make a movie, you have to have a script, and know how to tell a story well.

Work your way back. Write out the steps. Some will need a bunch of different levels under them. If you need to, do this on a huge piece of paper. Don't limit yourself! And definitely don't limit yourself because your paper isn't big enough. Write the steps out whatever way feels right: a list, a chart, a mind map, a tree diagram. It might even look like a big scribbled mess, but that's okay, because only you need to read it!

Let's keep going with that movie award: To have a script, you need to write one, or collaborate with a writer. To know how to tell a story well, you have to study film. To tell a story, you have to have life experience. To get life experience? Live life, take risks, and take note! To be able to tell a story well, you have to study movies...

When you accept your potential, and begin to dream as big as you can, ideas will begin to rattle around. Big and epic, or small and bizarre. Ask all of these ideas two questions. Does it make me happy? If it does, it stays. Then ask: Why not?

- ▶ A movie award. *Why not?*

- ▶ Because I haven't been nominated. *Why not?*

- ▶ Because I haven't made a movie. *Why not?*

Ask after every level. And put on your anything-is-possible hat and answer yourself (the hat is green!). The answer to 'Why not?' becomes your to-do list. For a little while, be a super-positive (probably super-annoying!) friend who always sees a way. You are clever and creative enough to do this. The question is, will you let yourself imagine a life with no limits? Will you let yourself be happy, even in your mind?

I can't get a movie award. *Why not?* Because I haven't made a movie. *So, make a movie...* I can't make a movie. *Why not?* I don't have an idea for a script. *So, do a brain dig of movie ideas! Make a plan, write a script!* But I don't have any gear to make a movie... *Go online, find a group of filmmakers, and join them. Or use your phone and edit online!* I wouldn't know where to start. *Start now, one step at a time. Let's find an article on how to write a movie script!*

Tackling why-nots solves problems and opens up possibilities. Hack at the why-nots until only the dream remains.

Once you know where you're heading, it can all become simple. Everything is possible. (And if you don't see a way, get together a roomful of extra brains to help you figure it out! We'll talk about this more in Scene Seven, when we recruit your army!) So, this is your plan. You want to take over the world? Cool! Just start now! Take charge! Create your own plan and act on it! We're done letting the current world tell us what's possible. Go through the steps of your plan. Ask yourself: What would someone need to do or have to get that? And write the answer underneath. At times it may splinter into several paths. Push on. Write it all down. Turn your 'Why not?' into 'What if?'

- ▶ What if you give it a go and it helps you find your way?

- ▶ What if you take a chance and it turns out to be amazing?

- ▶ What if everything works out beautifully?

You now have a kind of outline, a list of all the things you need to do to get where you want to be. Take this list, and pull it apart some more: What resources do you already have for each step? What tools or contacts do you need? How can you get them? Take the lower levels lower and lower, until something freaky happens...

- ▶ To study writing and film, I will need to do assignments.

- ▶ To do assignments, I need to enrol in a class.

- ▶ To enrol in a course, I need to research all available classes and select one.

- ▶ To research courses, I can go online now.

...suddenly you hit something that you can do now. Right now.

It's pretty amazing when you realize that you can put your foot on the path to exactly what you want this second. That when you open that book or go online today, you are carving out a direct link to your perfect world.

Catch your breath. Is your heart racing? Is your blood pumping? That is not your knees knocking, it's opportunity! So, don't stop there! Go up through the levels and work out when you can complete each step.

5 years from now.

4½ years from now.

4 years from now.

Complete over 3 years.

Begin next year.

This year.

2 weeks from now.

Today.

Now!!!

You now have a timeline. Put the actual dates on it, and drink in how doable this is! Feel the incredible deliciousness of being able to do something right now.

Blueprint Action: Aim!

1. Pick an area of your world. What does success look like for this area, this goal? Is it an object? A qualification? A feeling?

2. Use your imagination, and picture yourself there. Put yourself into your future.

3. What was the last thing you had to do to be in that moment? Write it down. Then ask, what was the last thing you had to do to be in this new moment?

4. Work your way back, writing everything down.

5. For each step, ask yourself: 'Does that make me happy?'

If it doesn't, either find another way to achieve it, or find a way to get excited about the step.

If it does, ask: 'Then why haven't I done this step yet? Why not?' The answer goes on your to-do list!

1. What do you need to do or get for each step or level?

---

2. Keep going back until you hit something that you can do now. Right now!

3. Add a timeline. This is doable!

4. Simplify your list and post it everywhere. You are on your way!

Blueprint Action: Aim! is your step-by-step plan. Your total blueprint. Keep a copy somewhere special and create a simplified version to use every day. Write out your destination, and the big steps that take you there. Then post it where you can relish it: your phone, your diary, your wallet, your car, your bathroom, and computer. Everywhere! Picture your success and cultivate an unstoppable desire! (I have a special hardcover notebook that inspires me when I see it.)

It's time to honour your sensitivities, to acknowledge your needs and be okay with who you are because, autistic or not, we're all playing the same game: Figure out your strengths. What do you love, what are you good at, what lights you up? That's where you belong. So, figure out exactly what success means to you. We're connected to the whole world. The rules are gone. If you want to write, write. If you want to publish, publish. But know this: You don't have to be able to speak, or write, or make eye contact to change the world. Any time you express yourself, any time you make the most of who you are, you change the world.

Because there is only one thing that is always true: You have something that no one else has, something valuable, special, and something that the world needs. It's your voice. Not your speak-up-in-class/small-talk/presentations voice. Your voice is the way you see the world. It's the way you live, the choices you make. Your voice is being who you are and sharing who you are. No masks, no Clark Kent glasses. You.

World domination isn't about masking our super, fitting in, or even changing the world, it's about finding the ways you can best serve the world with your strengths, with who you are. Know who you are, design your dream world, and make it happen.

And if you need to tone down the world? Wear headphones. Block out the sound. Wear the soft clothes. Stim. Speak. Medicate. Or don't. Do what you need to do to feel right in this world. Because it's not about fitting in, any more. It's about making the world your own. And yes, people will look. At first. Their eyes will register the difference. But their heart will too. And it will soften. Because this is the new world, and a label is not a prediction. This is your opportunity: to see what's possible in spite of and because of your diagnosis. It's time to stop trying to make autistics fit into the old world, and support us to create the new one!

As human mercury, triaging and processing is huge. I remember lying awake at night as a child, going over and over the day. What people said, what they did, colours, decisions, moments, all the things I had done wrong, what I would do differently next time. I was doing a kind of never-ending de-frag, looking for patterns, shuffling and filing my experiences to figure it all out. Every night I would fail, and every night I would start again, looking for the clues, the pieces, the answers. I didn't know then that was no solution, no answer. That I process things differently because I'm autistic, and even just knowing that, and knowing that it is *perfectly normal* for an autistic person, gives me permission to breathe.

It's already changing society moving forward, this kind of permission or allowing, which is actually just normalizing the things autistics are currently judged or criticized for. Stimming, pacing, looking away, eating food that is simple-safe-consistent. We've done it with headphones and weighted blankets. Things that were previously autistic neon signs are now seen as accessories for the stresses of modern life.

As autistic adults, in the same way that we have spent our lives fighting the signals our body sends us, we now get to rediscover our senses. To learn how to trust ourselves. Have you ever walked into a room and felt tension? Ever spoken with someone and known they were lying? Ever predicted something you couldn't have consciously known? Our environment sends us millions of signals, and thanks to our powerful sensing, filtering, and processing brains, we can draw conclusions and take actions. We've just spent so much of our time avoiding stress that we haven't taken advantage of our instincts. Autistics read and respond to the environment, it's just all coming at us at once. Learning to manage our energy will be a lifelong process, particularly in a world where energy out is business as usual, and energy in, self-care, is considered optional.

The Cassandra Complex is a metaphor based on Greek mythology. The God Apollo fell in love with the human Cassandra and gave her the gift of prophecy. However, when Cassandra turned down his advances, he added a curse: No one would ever believe her. Like many autistics, who pick up on data in the environment and can predict the consequences, Cassandra could see the future, but no one ever believed her. Autistics talk about holding and arranging information, finding patterns, seeing what others don't see. Many autistics report being the one who 'sees things coming', not through the gift of prophecy, but by simply spotting patterns and speaking truth. We are often criticized for being 'negative' but later proven right and resented for it. Denial is a powerful tool used by neurotypicals to protect them from an unwanted truth. Autistics value truth above self-preservation.

Now let's explore the flow of energy from an autistic point of view:

▶ *Energy in*: These are times of autistic joy, flow state, safety, recharge, time, space, being. Ways to bring energy in can include weighted vests or blankets, time by yourself, toys, arranging objects, napping, being in water, or stimming (more on this below). These are activities or actions that will be specific to the senses, sensitivities, and wiring of each individual but will always recharge, replenish, and refill energy.

▶ *Energy out*: These are demands that drain energy – sensory overwhelm, social overload, anxiety, camouflaging or masking (i.e. working to appear neurotypical) – and these autistic challenges are all on top of the flood of environmental data coming in – millions of bits of data from all our senses, that then have to be processed.

Autistics read, sense, and feel things that others don't. We have often grown up under intense gaslighting. We've been told 'You're too sensitive', 'No one else can feel it', 'It's not that bad/ not that loud/not that bright', etc. etc. The world will change when people stop trying to convince autistics that what they feel isn't real, and instead ask how these sensitivities can make the world better for everyone. All brains are affected by stress, all brains have ways of draining and replenishing energy. Autistics are just sensing it sooner, and more strongly. We are the canaries in the coal mine. But what if there is knowledge and power in our sensitivity?

Lots of autistics relieve stress and find joy in stimming. Stims can include:

▶ physical stims like clicking fingers, waving hands, clapping, rubbing, or pacing

▶ audio stims like humming, singing, or making or listening to sounds

▶ visual stims like colours, lava lamps, sand art, rainbows, or organizing objects

▶ tactile stims like fidgets, textured objects, or holding or touching materials.

Echolalia is the repeating, or echoing, of words and sounds. Autistics may use echolalia as a comforting stim (consciously or subconsciously), a way to feel grounded physically. We can also use echolalia as a communication strategy: scripts and shortcuts that repeat the patterns, vocabulary, and intonation of the words around us. To me, sometimes the way words sound together is an irresistible invitation to repeat them, as natural as calling out 'Polo' after 'Marco'.

Do you find yourself needing breaks from people? Social situations? Life? Lots of autistics find time with people (often even people that they love), and time in neurotypical environments, exhausting. This can be because of how hard we are working to mask and quietly white-knuckle through our stress.

There's a tipping point, energy demand outstrips supply. You can't spend energy without replenishing it, and this environmental overload can send autistics into meltdown, shutdown, or burnout. These are not tantrums, manipulations, attention-seeking, or naughtiness. They are all physical reactions to stress and overload.

There is no continuum 'more autistic' to 'less autistic'; it's more like a fulcrum: high energy reserves can meet more demands, less energy reserves fewer demands. But we are all individuals with different skills, strengths, and challenges. Our personal energy levels, strengths, supports, and priorities, *plus* the current environment, determines our ability to function at any time. Autistic + environment = ability to function.

> ## Blueprint Action: Energy In/Energy Out 🎬
>
> How does the flow of energy work for you? Start noticing what fills you with energy, and what drains you.

Since revealing my diagnosis to the world with the TEDx talk, I've been giving presentations on what life will be like when autistics are in charge (*Autistic World Domination* in Singapore and *When Autistics Rule the World* in Budapest). I speak about the advantages of autism and the ways that our world will benefit. Since that time, COVID-19 has arrived and changed our world in so many ways. Suddenly, many of the benefits of an autistic-friendly lifestyle have become compulsory:

- ► Flexible and work-from-home options have become acceptable, sometimes even ideal.

- ► Daily life has slowed down. Less rush, chaos, and noise.

- ► Routine is becoming more important. Not the clock-watching scheduled kind, the different rhythms of the day such as energy, weather, and mealtimes.

- ► Connecting in more conscious and meaningful ways. Ways that are less physical, less automated. We are okay to not be okay.

- ► Outings have become more purposeful and efficient, leaving the house now feels more significant.

- ► More written communication. No instant, emotion-reading response necessary. You can answer emails in your own time, respond to social media if/when you want to. (And guess what? You have unlimited hearts and Likes to give away!)

- ▸ The world is smaller, we care for strangers because there are no strangers really. This is a calmer, quieter, more conscious world. With a greater focus on what's important, increased (non-physical) connection, and greater appreciation and empathy without judgement.

Many autistics and neurodivergents thrive in a pandemic because after a lifetime of sucking up the realities of an unfriendly world, we already have fluid adaptation nailed. Rhythms and routine come naturally; strict rules are ideal. I already prefer working overnight, when the world becomes quiet, and my brain relaxes into icy-laser-focus. This benefits my clients too, meaning I often complete work in my time zone, finishing while they sleep.

Blueprint Action: The New World

What about you? What has the pandemic changed for you? New priorities? Perhaps deciding what to hold on to (connection?), or what to let go of (gossip?/a housemate?). It's definitely time to let go of the binary idea of success, the tunnel vision that says success is married, career, mortgage. The tunnel vision that says people must make small talk, and eye contact. We get to choose and create the world we want.

You have the dream, the vision, and the plan. Savour your wins, no matter how small, and enjoy each step. Every time you hit a target, congratulate yourself. You are getting closer and closer. The key now is action. Take a little action every day that pulls you towards the next step. And be open to making changes. At some point, a work goal may collide with a friendship goal.

Be flexible. Flow where life takes you. Your blueprint can take you from this very moment to your dream. But even dreams can change. Your life can be spun around in a flash. Be ready to switch plans if your heart pulls you somewhere else. You know what? Your happy ending changes all the time! Something in life may grab you in a new way. Be open to the universe giving you a hint, a nudge, or a shove. This is all about you.

So, there it was: the big red dot. I knew I would have to be brave, the bravest I had ever been. The most vulnerable, the most exposed. To speak the words, for the first time, publicly: 'I am autistic.' I knew it would be epic. But I didn't know it would be like *that*.

I slept for five days after the talk. The combination of fear, vulnerability, sensory overload, and adrenalin was exhausting. But I was proud. People listened, they nodded, they laughed at my jokes; and they did something that I never expected – they cried. I still receive incredible messages from people who say they recognize themselves or a loved one up on stage with me.

Autism is not a disorder or a deficit. It is a community, a culture, a way of being, and, yes, a disability – because in a world designed by and for typical brains, neurodivergents will continue to require supports to thrive. In the next scene we will explore the energy cost to being this way in a world designed for others. But for now? Know that world domination is possible with a plan that takes you from this very moment to your greatest dream. (Just remember that your happy ending changes all the time!)

Energy and Fire

Einstein. Mozart. Tesla. Some of the greatest minds to have graced planet earth were suspected autistics. Their bold thinking and unorthodox styles astounded the norms of their time but blazed a trail for the tools and technologies that are now commonplace.

What kinds of things used to be wild? Impossible? Things like running water? Electricity? A little box on your benchtop that can answer any question you ask?

Things often look crazy until they are done. In the beautiful words of Canadian writer and TV producer Brianne James, 'I am my ancestors' wildest dreams.' You know what that means? It means that we are the ancestors for future generations, right here, right now. We plant seeds for what now seems impossible. Our wildest dreams are on track to be embodied in our children, and in our children's children. We are the game changers.

Yes, you can take action this second that will lead you directly to your dream. But that doesn't make the dream your life. Once you have world domination, it dawns on you: right now is all we have. Your life is made up of each and every step on the path. Because no matter how much time we spend dreaming or planning our perfect world, our life is in this moment.

I'll show you. Go there now, to the place you're dreaming of.

You're accepting your award, cashing the cheque, celebrating world peace, and it goes like this: You're in. You've followed your blueprint. You've obliterated obstacles and taken on challenges. You are sitting where you've always wanted to be. You are doing what made you roll your eyes in the opening scene. You have achieved what you wanted, and you are ready to explode with happiness and power. This is your reality check. You make a mental list of the people who have supported you, so you can thank them. You go out and inspire people to do what you've done. You speak to groups, write letters of support, a book, or a blog. You pave the way for others to follow. You support charities and people that uplift your spirits. You make a difference!

And then it occurs to you. You always made a difference. From the time you entered the world, to right this moment sitting in your skin. You affect the people around you. You affect the world. Everything you do, and everything you don't do. By making someone smile, changing someone's mind, kicking off a dream, or ending a relationship, you send out ripples that change the world. Have you heard of the butterfly effect? It's the idea that a small thing in one place can create a big change somewhere else. Imagine that this is true. The world is so sensitive that a butterfly flapping its wings in New Zealand can create a sun shower in Las Vegas. That you make a difference, right this second. Whether you mean to or not.

Deep down (and not so deep down) you know this. You know this because it has been true all your life. Think of all the little things that have brought you here. You remember the teacher who said you could do anything; you remember the shop assistant that gave you the toy from the register because your eyes lit up when you saw it. You remember the kind words; you remember the harsh ones. These moments were fleeting but for some reason stayed with you, they taught you about the world and the people in it. You thought they taught you about yourself.

'Why can't it just be about the skating?' This line in the 2017 movie *I, Tonya* (directed by Craig Gillespie) so perfectly describes for me the frustration of being judged by your ability to fit in, rather than your ability to do the work. The movie is based on the turbulent life of Tonya Harding, an ambitious competitive ice skater. In the scene, Tonya is frustrated at being blocked for success in the skating competitions. She confronts the judge and he confirms it: she is being marked low; not because of her skill, work, or talent, but because she doesn't *look* or *act* a certain way. *'Tonya, it's never been entirely about the skating... you just refuse to play along.'*

Play along. Be normal. Fit in.

Sometimes, it doesn't matter how hard you work or how good you are: you don't fit. You. So, you've gone as far as you can go in this company, this group, this situation. No matter how good your work is. Because you don't say what they want to hear, you don't smile, you don't play along or make things easy. You don't lie. And it sucks. Office politics, social games, all of the weird-peopley-stuff on the edges – the things that should be icing but for some reason (society, time, history, and habit) seem to be cake.

Now, this could be my autistic thinking, but seriously, what does it matter what Tonya wears if she can land a triple axel? What does it matter if I don't go to after-work drinks if my writing is excellent? Who cares what I wear if my work ethic is bang-on? (Yes, I can hear myself. I know this stuff matters in the neurotypical world because it just does. Because it's the way it's always been. Because image and tradition and and and *and*. Because people.) I know I'm supposed to accept it. You can ace the work, nail the interview, be the best... but the people stuff matters. Because people make decisions based on emotion, not logic. Suddenly, you're left out of things, the conversations, the invitations, the projects, the promotions, because you don't play the game.

I've fought hard to fit in places that didn't fit me. I thought if I worked hard enough, if I changed, if I figured out the ways that I was broken and fixed myself, I would fit. I've wondered: If I was more qualified, more experienced, if I could prove my worth more fully – would it make a difference? I want to be good at what I do, I care about being accurate, truthful, and ethical – but now I know that my standards have to come from me and be for me. People often prefer likeable over competent, fun or easy over right – and that's okay. Those just aren't my people.

The skating. That's what should matter. In competitions. In life. What you do, not how you look. Who you are, not whether you fit. Because what if it's not you that's wrong? What if this is just a signpost directing you to the right? Helping you to find where you belong? Right you, wrong place.

Blueprint Action: Feel Your Way

Here's the advice:

- If you can possibly help it, follow the happy feelings. Know that the places and people that are right for you will feel good.

- If it feels wrong, trust yourself. Look for alternatives, plot your escape. Keep looking.

- Figure out your strengths. What do you love, what are you good at, what lights you up? That's where you belong.

- Work on your flexibility: remember it's not all or nothing. You can keep your day job (for now!) and write your screenplay at night. You can get through your online training module to get to your band practice. You can create your dream world bit by bit.

Have you ever had your life interrupted by a nyeugh? Not a big red flag, or a flashing neon sign, just a little nyeugh? A nyeugh might be a feeling in your stomach, a phrase you keep hearing, or a leg that keeps getting bruised in the same place. A nyeugh usually starts small, but when it gets ignored, it grows.

It's easy to brush off a nyeugh, it's like the lunch bell at school; the bell can tell you it's time to stop and refuel, but it can't force you to actually eat. Not at first. At first, a nyeugh is just a message, a signal that maybe something needs to happen or to stop happening. After that, it will escalate into a growling stomach, a foggy brain, or even an impromptu nap. So, what if a nyeugh in your body is a call to action? What if your heart is telling you things without words? And what if you started to listen?

All my experiences feeling wrong have made it easier to know when something is right. And I don't want it to be this way for my kids. I don't want that to be this way for anyone. If I could go back? I would look more quickly for the signs that I didn't fit, and be grateful. I wouldn't waste time or energy trying to squeeze myself into the wrong box – I'd create my own world – the one where I get to be me, do good work with good people who get me. It's possible, believe it! Insist on it!

Our children are the miracle, and we need to reshape the world for them. Meanwhile, keep your awesomeness where it's appreciated. Stay with places and people that celebrate your strengths and build on your positives, and do the same for them. You can spend your whole life trying to fight your weaknesses, trying to convince people who don't get it, or you can spend your energy making magic with the one (or three, or six million) who do.

I had a job in an office for a while. I would be at my job and cry every day. And crying is cool – do it, do it everywhere – it's real, it's true, it's your body letting you know that you can't and shouldn't hold in your feelings. But if it's happening every day?

Sometimes it's not you, it's them. Love doesn't burn in your chest, happiness doesn't quake. If you are losing it, going off, shutting down, take notice. When you are doing the right thing, when you are in your world, your body is at peace.

How about this... From now on, you see not fitting in as a gift. A signpost directing you to where you do belong, where you do fit. We have got to stop looking outside ourselves to figure out who we are. Look in, feel in. Tune in to yourself. Where's your energy going? So much energy fitting in, listening so I say the right thing, watching so I can head off threats, trying to earn your approval, trying to earn my place. Stop looking for danger outside and trust your body, tune in to who you are. Float downstream. It is time to stop using our energy to adapt to the neurotypical world, it's time to create our own.

Sure, from the outside it's black and white. Don't like it? Leave! Crappy job? Get a new one! Bad boyfriend? Break it off! But the only place it's black and white is on the outside. You're up to your eyeballs in grey. You love the work but hate the system, your dream apartment is in another country, she's toxic but you love her... We need a new system. A system that gives us clarity, a system that makes decisions easy and obvious. How about this... If it's grey it's not perfect, and you deserve perfect. Completely perfect for you. And grey? Grey just means you're not sure. Yet. So, get sure. Get clear.

Autistics are known for literal communication. This means if you say 'Take a couple', I'll take two. If you say 'I'll be five minutes', I'll time it. Direct, honest, upfront. I follow instructions, I follow rules. I trust that people say what they mean and mean what they say. Spoiler alert: People seldom say what they mean or mean what they say. In lots of ways, your body is also very literal – it doesn't understand 'She doesn't mean it' or 'If I stay in this miserable job for another six months, I can leave'. Your body doesn't get buried in detail, it doesn't care about grey; your body just responds to how you feel in the moment.

Autistics change the game to live. To play. To be who we are. We are gamechangers because we have to be. And it's time to go to the next level.

Blueprint Action: Big Picture

Your life. You have limited years and limited energy. How will you spend it? From now on, make choices that support who you are and what makes you happy. For real. Consider where you will live, what you will do to earn money, how much free time you need to have to recover and replenish your energy.

Oh, and hey this is not a time for grizzling, 'should haves', or beating yourself up in any way. (I know, old habits, right?) Remember we're here for world domination! To design and create the perfect world *for you*. This is a clean slate, starting now. If you could have anything, with no limitations, what would you do, be, or have?

> *Career choices*: What do you love to do? What gives you energy? Do you like to work indoors or outdoors? With people or with information? With your hands or with computers? Narrow down the kinds of jobs and environments that give you energy.

> *Home choices*: Where do you want to live? In the city or the country? Close to public transport? Near friends or family? With a garden? Independently or with support?

Look through your blueprint. Do your goals consider the way you spend and replenish energy? Have you set goals with your energy in mind? Are there any areas that you could tweak to feel better?

The human body is designed beautifully and mysteriously, and even on the cutting-edge of medicine, we are still learning about the meat-suit we call home. We can pump our blood full of chemicals to numb ourselves, our hearts bang when our brains translate scary movies into a physical reaction. There are people like Kandinsky who experience synaesthesia, a blending of the senses, they see numbers as colours, hear art as music. If your body is tense, you probably are, too. And if your body is happy, chances are, so are you! So, pause, tune in, your body is speaking, are you listening?

Our greatest human gifts are time and energy. Let your nyeughs guide you towards what you really want, and what you actually deserve. What if we took all the energy we're spending trying to get our autistics to eat food that touches, look us in the eye, and pretzel themselves to fit into the current world, and spent it supporting them to find peace, to find passion, and to create the new world?

When we're little we are the most beautiful creatures in the world, and we know it. We are tiny, perfectly formed little people. Sure, if we were any other species, we'd have our own family. Instead, we spend much longer in the nest, ripening our brains for independence. And whether they mean to or not, everyone that comes into contact with us can have an influence on who we might become.

Millions of people, moments, words, and actions have affected your life. Do you know what that means? It means that your words and actions have affected the lives of others. You communicate with every cell. Every moment you exist. You can't help it. You can't stop it. You ooze who you are and what you believe. When you spend time with people, everything you do is absorbed, and whether people remember it consciously or not, it helps shape who they are. And when you don't spend time with the people you care about? They know you're not there. They know that you missed that birthday, that phone call, that meeting. Whether it's because you're busy, sick, working, tired, or it's the season finale of *Survivor*, it doesn't matter – you send a message.

Without words or actions, you can change things. Your absence makes a difference; so, your very presence is a power. How you choose to wield that power will affect your experience of life, and the experiences of those around you. *And that's if you do nothing.*

Now, throw in your actions, your thoughts, your responses, your intentions... What if we are so much more important than we realize? What if every one of us is mind-blowingly, world-changingly powerful? In soft and subtle ways measured in frequency and vibration? If you knew that, would it make a difference? Ask yourself. And wait for the answer.

Listen to the part of you that is made of the same stuff as stars. The same stuff as Shakespeare. That part knows for sure that you are special, that your life has a purpose greater than anything you can imagine. That's the only part worth listening to.

To me the question is what makes me happier – believing that I was born special or believing that I don't make a difference? Hey, there's evidence for both. But only one makes me feel good. And it's the 'what if' that pushes me to be bigger than myself. Because what if, like Superman, everyone is born with powers to discover and grow into? And what if, like Batman, everyone has resources to uncover and utilize?

When we become the superhero we were born to be, our world is shaped around us. We also change the worlds of the people in our lives.

If someone speaks to me harshly, I can't focus on anything else until it's sorted. If you knew that your tone could set me worrying for the weekend, would you still do it? Or what if you knew that your sweetness could have me bouncing off the ceiling for a week? Would it make a difference?

You can make people feel good with a smile or a thoughtful gesture. You have that infinite power. Holding the door for someone can change their day, kind words can change their life. I find it hard to accept praise, but when something gets through, I treasure it like a jewel. I admire it, tuck it away, and bring it out when I feel dark. If I think I can give that gift to someone else, I don't hesitate. I make a difference, and I know that because you make a difference to me.

Blueprint Action: Millions of Moments

1. Think of the moments in your life when other people have helped you to feel really good. Happy, connected, loved, excited. Think of big moments and little ones. They all count!

2. Notice how good you feel just remembering them. If you can't think of any, try imagining some - your brain won't know the difference! An imagined kiss can feel as good as a real one!

3. Find ways to make other people feel good. Big and little.

Time flies. And you will change the world. Not because of what you do for a job, or how much you earn, but because in all the time you exist there will be millions of moments where you send messages. With what you say and don't, with what you do and don't.

Once you are dominating your world, the things you do are magnified. Do things that make you proud. And do things that make the world better. But know that you change the world in every moment.

When you send kindness out, it comes back to you. It ripples and multiplies. It grows, it bounces back. This is how you change the world. Little by little, big by big, starting now! Don't wait to be rich or famous or anything else, change the planet. You're doing it now.

You are creating your perfect world. Let's go deeper. Because while your goals describe what you want and where you're going, your intentions take you to the next level! Your intentions are heartfelt, they explore how you will do things: how you will feel, how you will act. This is the way to bring power and magic to every moment, to make the most of your energy.

Blueprint Action: Your Intentions – Up, Up, and Away!

Take each area of your life and write out your intentions. For you, for the people you love, for the world! Then make intentions part of your life. Here are some snappy examples:

> Intend to have a sound sleep.

> Intend to have a productive study session.

> Intend to listen carefully to your friend.

Here are some meatier examples:

> *Relationships*: I will create win-win relationships by being true to myself and appreciating others. I will learn about myself through my relationships.

> *Spirituality*: Growing every day, I will learn to speak my truth. I will hold myself with awareness. I will hold myself with integrity and inner strength. I will find out who I really am.

Health: I will build a strong body and mind from the inside out. I will fill myself with happy food and positive thoughts. I will love the process!

Abundance: I will create abundance in my life by contributing to the world. By giving, not taking.

Love: I will create love in my world by giving love, and by appreciating the love that is given to me.

Success: I will succeed in my career by learning everything I can and looking for ways to make things better.

Your intentions are like your personal vision, they are just for you. So, when you write them, be honest, kind, and true.

In the end? One authentic social media post can touch someone, change them, with as much significance as an entire book. Your presence. Your actions and inactions. So, get your gold medal, write your book, go for your dreams, but know what success is for you. Because often your true dream can be achieved in many ways. For example, if you want to write a book to connect with people and make a difference, know that you can also do that with conscious presence or a heart-centred social media post.

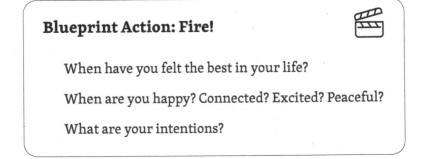

Blueprint Action: Fire!

When have you felt the best in your life?

When are you happy? Connected? Excited? Peaceful?

What are your intentions?

The fact that you exist gives you amazing power. You make a difference. Right now. In every moment that you breathe. In every moment that you live. You can't control what is absorbed, what is remembered, or what is appreciated, but you can control what you put out. You can spread bubbles, fizz, and oomph in any moment. You can change the world.

Autism-Friendly Is Human-Friendly

I'm in a complicated relationship with the supermarket. On the one hand, it is an unfathomable modern miracle, a logistical luxury that sees every kind of food imaginable weaving its way across the planet for the sole purpose of meeting me. The supermarket is beautifully lined-up labels, perfect tin pyramids, a long-aisled, shiny-floored, absolute abundance of items for me to buy or reject at will. It is a single location filled with more deliciousness than I could ever eat, let alone need. It is a tribute to human choice and privilege, it is an everyday extravagance, and an awe-inducing wonder.

On the other hand, ew! The supermarket is a nightmare. It is loudspeaker interruptions, rattling trolley wheels, flying numbers, peopley-people, ladders on wheels, mismatched products, social niceties, screechy radio, hurried parents, yelling fonts, a thousand decisions, and So. Much. Maths.

Do you remember when they first started 'quiet-hour' in the supermarkets? It was designed for autistics. To soften the sensory overload that leads many of us into meltdowns or shutdowns. Loudspeakers down, less shelf-stacking and movement, dimmed lights. One hour a week. A gesture, a token. But do you know what happened? Lots of neurotypical people were stirred by the change. Shoulders dropped; foreheads un-furrowed. They could breathe again. They felt the difference.

Bit by bit, we've let the environment heat up around us. We've forgotten that the world doesn't have to be so loud, bright, constant, and in-our-faces. We pinball from stress to stress, task to task, day to day. So, when things are quiet, it throws us. Jolts us. We're so used to the toxins that peace feels like poison. Our systems have adapted, but luckily, deep down in our bones, we remember. We remember what it means to be. To just be.

And as the world gets louder, neurodivergent people don't have the luxury of 'going with the flow', we're just not wired that way. We are sensitive to the rough and the mean. We are foreign to the world we're born into. So we kick, we thrash. The older autistics, the ones obscure and undiagnosed, we hid and blamed ourselves. But the new ones? They flip tables, they go mute, they fight to be heard. And? Their parents are listening. Their teachers are learning. Changes are being put in place in offices, workspaces, schools, and homes. It's happening, slowly. People are getting it, becoming more sensitive and aware. People are making changes not only because it 'ticks the diversity box' but because what works for autistics works for all people. Autism-friendly is human-friendly.

Neurodivergence is increasing across the population. Greater awareness, increased education, dissolving stereotypes, access to diagnosis. Difference is the new normal. This openness and desire for diversity is changing the way workplaces run, and with the right systems, attitudes, and innovations has the potential to open the entire world up even more – to boost the happiness and satisfaction of all people, even the neurotypicals.

The statistics say more than 80 per cent of autistics are underemployed,[8] and it's not because we don't have the skills, qualifications, talent, will, or work ethic. We often don't work because the current systems are designed by and for regular brains. And they can make us (often literally) sick. Those of us who have survived have either done it by striking out on our own, or by dealing with our discomfort at a huge personal cost.

And then came COVID-19. And suddenly the world was plunged into a reality where 'normal' became: physical isolation, increased routine, non-touchy communication. For many people, autistics, neurodivergents, this 'new' normal was our 'always normal'. The old world was designed for the majority, if you wanted to live outside the box you had to build it first. Many of us already work from home, don't drive, and have a (super) tight social circle. In the time of a pandemic – globalization, conserving time and energy, sudden and epic change – we're more conscious, more kind, we use technology to care for each other. The pandemic didn't create these ideas, it just made them necessary. The pandemic provided a speed of change that gave organizations the freedom (or the desperation if you like) to adapt. To make work from home possible, desirable, for organizations to bend in new ways. And suddenly? We can change the world from our comfort zone, fresh voices are connecting and being heard, some for the first time.

The Social Model of Disability says that people are disabled by a world that is not set up to accommodate their differences. For example, a person isn't disabled because they use a wheelchair, but because their workplace does not have access ramps. Translate that to neurodivergencies: We are disabled by environments built for typical brains. So, what happens when classrooms allow headphones or sensory and movement breaks? What happens when job interviews focus less on first impressions, and more on trial work performance?

As an autistic, you don't have to identify as disabled (and that's your choice). But just know that when autism is recognized as a disability, it supports and validates the struggles of many other autistics. It also means the people who need supports are more likely to access them. Personally, I struggle with internalized ableism (see box), I resisted being diagnosed as autistic, but when I heard that autism is a disability? I denied that label completely. I interpreted 'disabled' as a description that meant broken or less-than, someone to be pitied. I already felt weak and inferior, and to me, identifying as disabled made it real, and because I appeared average on the outside, I felt like a fraud as well. Now, I am comfortable identifying as disabled, because I know that it just means the current world is not designed to meet my needs. Now, I know that just because I *can* push through, it doesn't mean I *should*, and that if there are supports or strategies available, taking them doesn't make me weak, it makes me human.

Ableism is discrimination based on the belief that people with typical abilities are superior. It can be as blatant as insults, and as subtle as a stereotype. Ableism is seeing people with disabilities as damaged or expendable, and disability as something to fix rather than something that just is. Like racism, sexism, and ageism, ableism is insidious and can seep through in language, attitudes, and behaviours. *Internalized ableism* is when we project that ableism onto ourselves. For example, comparing ourselves to others, thinking we are inferior, defective, or not disabled 'enough' to deserve supports (basically my exact reaction to finding out autism is a disability).

The American social justice activist Talila A. Lewis has a working definition of ableism[9] that addresses gaps in the traditional framing:

A system of assigning value to people's bodies and minds based on societally constructed ideas of normalcy, productivity, desirability, intelligence, excellence, and fitness. These constructed ideas are deeply rooted in eugenics, anti-Blackness, misogyny, colonialism, imperialism, and capitalism. This systemic oppression that leads to people and society determining people's value based on their culture, age, language, appearance, religion, birth or living place, 'health/wellness,' and/or their ability to satisfactorily re/produce, 'excel' and 'behave.' You do not have to be disabled to experience ableism.*

Disability does not describe a person, it expresses support requirements to navigate the current world. Disability is determination and innovation. In a fully accessible world, not only is there no disability, but all people thrive. Let's add to this, that over the course of a human lifetime, we will all experience support needs – from reading glasses to pregnancy, mobility challenges, even a broken finger will suddenly show you the value of a thoughtful environmental adjustment. Disability can be permanent or temporary, visible or invisible. Human needs are universal, and acknowledging our needs is empowering.

> When a disability can't be seen, it is known as a *hidden disability* or *invisible disability*. For example, people with chronic pain, brain injury, or learning differences. Like autism, invisible disabilities mean a person can be seen as lazy or weak, when we are actually working really hard.

Imagine if organizations were conscious of meeting human needs. Across brains, bodies, and abilities. What if they actively looked for ways to preserve and enhance the time, strengths, and energy of every individual heart and mind they nurture?

---

* For deeper understanding, you can read more about TL's work on their website: www.talilalewis.com.

As simple as wider doorframes to ease life for mobility scooters, pushchairs, and manoeuvring. Or as complex as individualized working environments, to acknowledge the sensory-softening or sharpening options unique to each person. Universal design puts the focus on creative tailored solutions, not efficiency or conformity.

Blueprint Action: The Universal Human

Consider supports that would make your life easier. (And notice that this is not about whether you 'need' it, because chances are you've gone your whole life without help. This isn't about need. We don't have to need help to want it, deserve it, or get it!)

Headphones	Weighted lap pad or blanket	Fidget items
Wobble stools	Hammocks	Activity breaks
Walking desks	Soft, controllable lighting	Captioning
Physical spaces	Time flexibility	Technology
Career guidance	Note-taking assistance	Mentoring
Quiet spaces	Hands-on learning options	Work from home

And if you've never tried sensory-friendly, autism-friendly items? Try them! Even the ideas that seem silly can be life-changing. Give yourself the opportunity to feel better, to be better. What if the very traits and sensitivities we have pathologized are actually opening new pathways to human success?

That's what's possible. A normal that not only reflects reality, because neurodiversity is already reality, but also boosts and superpowers exactly who we are. Because we focus on our strengths and look for ways to tweak our environment. Better and better, because we are worth that.

My profession, my trade, is writing. I love absorbing and transforming technical information. Science, computing, cat grooming, business. For every subject, the keys are the same: break it down, find the connections, make it fun. Feeling the words click into place, going into flow state, where the world disappears, and I'm filled with energy and drive. When I'm writing I feel more myself than at any other time, and being able to do it for a living is a dream I will never take for granted. My favourite time-spend, alone, in the dark, human contact via email. And since my comfort zone is home alone, I've been pretty much living outside the box to do what I love. (And guess what, neurotypical naysayers? I don't need social skills, eye contact, or fresh air to do it.)

Autistics change the game to thrive, and that lets everyone see success in new ways. Is the point to do beautiful work? Or is the point to do the work the way it's always been done? And is the point to be happy? Or is the point to be happy the way everyone else is doing it?

There is no one way, no right way. There is, however, a growing realization that neurodivergence brings innovation. That the future will be built by the people who already see it, the people itchy in the current world, motivated to create a new one because in many ways they are already there.

It's time to change the way we define success. It's not necessarily: degree, marriage, mortgage. The divorce rate is high, people burn out at jobs they hate, and meanwhile there are a whole lot of happy single people living in their parents' basement. There's only one person in the world that you need to make happy, and coincidentally, only one person in the world that you have complete control over. Everyone else has their own world to dominate, their own blueprint they're working on.

Get ready. Your army starts with you! You are the leader. You set the example, and you lead the way. Just because you're only in control of one person, it doesn't have to mean you're on your own. You can build an army that will work with you, and make your world smoother, easier, and all the more possible! You decide who you want on your team and as part of your world. And you know what? You already have an army! You probably just don't call it that.

Your friends, family, advisers, role models – they are your army! Your army is made up of the people who give you what you need. It can be hundreds of online followers, or one inspiring friend. It can be a character, a celebrity, or a close-knit family. Whatever works for you! Think about your world, are there people in your life right now that inspire or support you?

Blueprint Action: Your Army

1. Who is in your army right now? Friends? Family? Teachers? A boss? A therapist? Characters in a book? Your online followers? Toys? Pets? A celebrity?

2. How do these people support your world? Do they inspire you, give you advice, praise you, keep you on track, or something else?

3. You may like to collect photos or images of these people. Admire your army. Know that you are supported in your world. Let their names or pictures show you that you can do anything.

Right now, in your town, there are people making their dreams come true, people having fun, working smart, and living their dreams. You may shop at their store, or walk past their construction site, you might read about them online, or hear about awards that they've won. Start thinking: Is there anyone else you want to include in your army? Go out, hunt around. And always, always look for people who love what they do. You can learn more from the waiter who treats customers as family than the restaurant owner who dreads coming in to work. Job title means nothing, attitude is everything.

The whole world is at your fingertips. Real, imagined, and online! All around you, there are people who are where you want to go, people with strengths you can learn from. If you have a question, there's an answer – your army is everywhere!

Once you identify someone, kick into gear! Talk to them, email, tell them they have a skill you admire, tell them you want to know their secret. This will not only make them feel great (imagine if someone asked you!), but their response may be a jewel that you use for the rest of your life. Let people know that you're super-keen, get in their faces with your talents and your needs. When you ask for help, the universe opens up.

As people, we are soooo much more than our titles and resume. We are the heart, the spark, the energy of a home or business. And now organizations are starting to create and hold spaces – physical, mental, and emotional spaces – for neurodivergencies with all of their strengths, challenges, and delicious difference. Seriously. There are companies who make an autism diagnosis a prerequisite of working with them. They make sensory adjustments, rearrange workspaces, they prioritize being autism-friendly. Software companies, animation studios, factories, and corporate offices. Because in the right environment, autistics are loyal, hardworking, honest employees. We're great at repetitive tasks, error spotting, problem solving. We don't lie, we don't pretend, we don't take as many sick days.

Smart employers are catching on and using a diagnosis as a way of finding the best employees. No kidding. Money is being spent to analyse and take advantage of making neurodivergent brains more comfortable. Obviously, there's plenty of room for debate in this space, but for now, I'm happy to see our strengths being recognized and opportunities for autistics are flooding in.

You might not be seeing this in your town (or even your country) right now, but globally? There are organizations actively supporting and celebrating our differences for the strengths they bring, as people and professionals. This is a revolution that puts humanity at its molten-hot core. This is a future that will see being multiply divergent as an edge in work and in life. Start seeing it for yourself and be part of getting to the yes!

Getting to the yes can mean different things. It can mean getting the love, getting the job, or just getting in the door. Your yes might come from a parent or friend, an employer, or a receptionist. Your yes could bring you one step closer, or it could land you smack-bang in the place you've been dreaming of. It doesn't matter who, what, when, or why – but getting to the yes is up to you!

Blueprint Action: Get to the Yes

1. Look for people or organizations that match the different areas of your blueprint. For example:

   ▷ Want to work with animals? Check out a vet, the zoo, or the RSPCA.

   ▷ Want to get into publishing? Find a local writer, go to the library, or jump online.

2. Does anything spark a passion or curiosity for you?

3. Make contact! Ask questions, learn more!

Many of the people and places you've identified will be more than happy for you to go in and check out what they do. There may even be opportunities for interning, life experience, or who knows what! And remember, there's always more than one way to shell a jellybean! The first business says no? Try another, then another. You can't make anyone do anything, but you can knock on doors until the right one opens.

There is always a way. Shrug off the nos, they are temporary. This is your world. In your world there is only yes. It won't always be without conditions, but you will always have a choice.

Building an army reminds you that even though there are plenty of people who'll tell you that you can't, there are also a whole heap who will tell you that you can. Know that there are hundreds of ways around everything. And everything is possible for you! You can study, you can learn on the job, you can build an army, and you can take over the world. Whether you're twelve, twenty, or one hundred and two; you can start absolutely anything, right now!

Look for your people. They are out there. People who will back you, support you, love you. Give yourself the opportunity to find your people, by shining so they can't miss you. Here are some ideas:

- *Volunteer*: Join groups that will involve you with a range of people, or support causes that interest you. Learn about organizations in your community that make a difference. You'll find that the most interesting people usually have the most intense schedules. And people who are willing to give their time and gifts to help others are respected for it. They often have connections that can support your mission, and qualities that you can absorb.

Plus, there's that cool way the universe tends to look after people who care about others!

- ▶ *Experiment*: You have precious time and energy reserves, and you can give yourself permission to try things! What's it like to work with animals? With kids? In an office? Scooping ice cream? Another great thing about being autistic is that we tend to know fairly quickly, accurately, and emphatically what we don't like. Trying things can be a great way to start knocking out what you don't want in your world!

- ▶ *Study*: Find inspiration and motivation in the stories of others. Read about people who have the lives that you dream of, analyse their success, learn from their mistakes. Watch movies about people who inspire you. Use the experience of others to figure out how to overcome obstacles and handle criticism, to show yourself what's possible!

You might hear 'No', 'Impossible', 'It can't be done', and all the rest of the crap that some people want you to believe. You can't take this personally. First, because it distracts you from your own world, and second, because it's not about them. Everyone else is working on their own goals. They're not rejecting you or your ideas because it gives them an evil thrill; you are just not meeting the needs that they have at this time.

How people react to you often has nothing to do with you. If they have a problem with you, your idea, your passion, the way you dress, or the way you talk, it's just that – their problem. You never know what you're walking into when you deal with people. You could go for a job interview the day the manager finalizes her divorce, or email a business when their system is down. You can only control you. So, negotiate, adapt, be creative, and be persistent. There are opportunities everywhere!

You can learn something from every person and every situation when you are curious, interested, and open-minded.

Persistence can be a powerful tool. And super-persistence comes from super-desire. The passion to keep going, no matter what gets thrown in your way. World domination can ignite this super-desire. What's more important than making the world your own? (Answer: Nothing! You've probably already spent way too long hiding who you are and what you want, it's time to put you first!) And persistence isn't just about trying and trying and trying again, it's about creativity, problem solving, finding alternatives, working smart, believing in yourself, and believing in your goals.

You can only control how you live your life. Remember, everyone else is on the same planet but not in the same world. Don't be thrown. Be ready for anything. Because (surprise!) there is no 'real' world. Your world is real for you, like everyone else's is real for them. You decide what is acceptable in your world, what is real, what is happy. No one can tell you how the world is because the world is defined as you go. People can tell you what they have experienced, or how it has been for them. But how the world is now? How it's going to be? These things you decide. And you do this by hunting out the people who won't try to tell you how the world is, but will help you make the one you want.

Oh, and sucky people? Lots of people straight out suck. You've probably met lots of them already, and you might even meet a whole lot more. Only one thing makes this okay. Sucky people can bring you closer to the world you want, by showing you the one you don't want. But this part? It's lifelong learning. We're especially vulnerable to sucky people because, as autistic humans, our instinct is to tell the truth. We tend to be generous, trusting, open, and believe that others are the same.

There's this idea floating around that autistics can't lie. That we'll say the thing that everyone is thinking. That we're blunt, rude, obnoxious (aka direct, honest, trustworthy). Like everything with autism, there's a spectrum: some of us can't lie, some of us won't, some can lie but we're really bad at it, some of us have figured out tact the hard way, and most of us are still learning.

For me, I've lost a lot for saying what I see as matter of fact/ the truth. Family, friends, experiences, so much money. For me, there was the time I told someone, 'I forgive you, but now I can't trust you as far as I can throw you.' (Okay, but I figured we both knew she lied, so obviously I couldn't trust her any more. I knew it, she knew it. I even made it a joke to lighten the mood. Why are people offended by the truth?) (I know now that I probably should've stopped talking after the forgiving part. Hindsight, right?)

There was also the time I turned down a work contract, because I wasn't happy with the values of the company. They responded by offering me more money. We went back and forth three times. They thought I was negotiating. I wasn't. I didn't want to work for them. And even if I did, why would I lie to push someone to recognize my value and offer more money? You offer what the work is worth, I accept or decline. It would never occur to me to turn something down as a way to get more money, and it never occurred to them that no amount of money would change my mind. This kind of neurotypical gameplaying is confusing, unnecessary, plus totally favours the overconfident (and probably incompetent).

You'll often find autistics calling people out. Saying things are not okay. Saying something is wrong and being the only one who will say it. I've had people ask me to speak up (because they know I can't not), thank me for it, but never back me up publicly. And I don't blame them. Doing the right thing doesn't always feel good. And actually? I've found that telling the truth hardly ever feels good. They say people shoot the messenger for a reason. I've always been honest, not because I thought it would score me points or make anyone like me, it's always felt like I can't not. I can't be the one who knew and didn't say. Even when they hate you for it. Little picture, that's sad. Big picture, that's not sad. Yay for the autistic kids that haven't learned to put filters on, yay for the people brave enough to tell the truth because they want a better world.

Anyway. For me telling the truth usually just feels matter of fact, or necessary. Less like 'I have to say something' and more like 'I can't not say something'. Less like 'I'm a champion of truth and justice' and more like 'I will not sleep at night if I let this go on'. And it sucks. Ideally, you'd be able to apply some thinking to it before you speak up: 'Hmmm, is this in my best interests? What consequences am I likely to experience if I speak out?' 'How will people react once they know I feel strongly and won't budge?' Ideally. But life isn't ideal, and being autistic isn't a choice.

As adults, we've probably learned a lot of this the hard way. Adult autistics report broken relationships and confusing interactions that have followed them as long as they can remember. Because of this, many of us push people away before they can hurt us, or build a wall to protect ourselves. This is another reason masking hurts so much. We're caught between wanting to be ourselves and wanting to be loved. I wish there was an easy answer. People stuff is just hard. It's hard even when your brain *does* come pre-loaded with all the right social moves. But when you're autistic? It's boss-level hard. So, what do we do? Focus on what you have. One friend? A brother who gets you? A cat that listens to your stories? Someone online that you connect with? Appreciate the good people. Acknowledge the big things, the little things, and especially the things that no one else notices. Thank people on paper, in person, with words or with presents. Not because that's how you get or keep friends, but because appreciation speaks to the universe. Everyone loves to be noticed and appreciated, and your kindness might change the world for them.

Your world is up to you, and your army is made up of the people who help you shine. Find opportunities, and milk them for all they're worth. Build your army. Your yes might be the next person you talk to, the next email you send, the next door that you knock on. People can say no, but you don't have to hear it. They can say you can't, but you don't have to prove them right. Push through, keep moving, drive ahead. Get to the yes!

More and more, organizations are looking to adapt to neurodivergent brains. By showing up as your authentic self, by figuring out and explaining the ways you work best, you rewrite normal. Inclusion means we can get to every individual's strengths faster, we can focus on the what and the why, because the how...? The how is an environment where accessing support and having needs met is upfront and simple.

If accessibility and inclusion were universal, there would be no disability. So, let's stop creating tools, environments, classrooms for the typical human, the majority, the normal, the least-needy, and start creating for the universal human. The universal human isn't less-than, they are possibilities, they have choices. There are no special needs. There are needs. Learning needs, support needs, human needs. And what if we put those supports in place, so well, so universally, that they are no longer supports but the default setting? Imagine if accessibility wasn't boxes to tick but a fully inclusive way of working and being? This would allow all people to thrive, neurodivergent or not. We have more information and technology that we've ever dreamed of. Let's redefine what it means to be human.

Scene Eight

The Bridge Builders

I was six years old, and the top of the fridge was like the top of a mountain. Mum and Dad were still asleep, and if I kept my movements slow and soft, they would stay asleep. I opened the pantry cupboard door; from here, I could pull myself up onto the bench and reach Dad's special box. In the box he had his cigarettes, lighters, wallet, and my target: his tiny Māori books. He had shown them to me before, full of warnings to 'be careful', and 'they're not toys'.

I am autistic, I am Māori, but like many indigenous and neurodivergent people, I wasn't empowered with my identity as a child. The tiny Māori books represented a part of me that was special, but locked away. Not for playing with or showing off. I am Māori, indigenous, magical – but colonization is insidious. One thousand years after my ancestors navigated by the stars to make a home in Aotearoa, New Zealand, and colonization has meant that not only are we fighting to preserve our language, our stories, and our way of life, and not only are many of us disconnected from our roots, but also? Many of us still quietly, shamefully, hate ourselves for who we are. Not good enough. Not white enough, but not Māori enough either.

But it only takes a seed. Language, hope, tiny books of words. For me, the seeds were that my dad kept and treasured those little Māori *taonga*, treasures. That he told me our ancestors were Māori, and he said it with pride. Seeds like these hold tight in your heart, and wait.

When you're a kid, you don't need to know everything. You take the bits and pieces you have, and you build the story that makes the most sense. I knew I was smart and full of feelings, I knew I was weird, I knew I was Māori. But I wasn't smart enough to be normal. And I didn't look like other Māori. And I cried so much that people had stopped asking me why. I was never diagnosed with anything, I never met anyone like me. So, all I knew for sure was that I was different, and I was alone. So, I spent most of my life trying to disguise how I felt and who I was, because the only thing worse than being different? Being found out.

'You can't be Māori – you're too white.' Scenes repeated in the playground and the classroom until I stopped telling people I was Māori. I wasn't raised with strong links to my culture, and raised in a time, a place, where internalized racism dug its claws in and settled. So, like the little Māori books, my culture stayed in a box. Special but hidden. Like being autistic, my Māori identity was mine to share or conceal. I had the privilege, and the curse, of passing for white, allistic, and average.

When I was diagnosed autistic, I went through a long period of anger and denial. I read everything. All the things I couldn't do, shouldn't do. All the things that, by medical definition, I am supposed to find difficult at best, impossible at worst. Working, driving, being in a relationship. And it freaked me out. I mean, if I'm not supposed to be driving, should I be driving? And if I'm not supposed to be married, should I let my husband know?

I knew I could keep up the normal act, life as usual. There are plenty of reasons to keep it quiet: denial, fear, prejudice, judgement, rejection (and that's just in my head!). Why rock the *waka*? I've made it this far; I've pulled off normal my entire life, why tell now?

Then I realized: People are being diagnosed now, today. And these parents and newly diagnosed autistics are being fed the same lies and limitations ('autistics always...' and 'autistics never...'), and these words are poison. Because if the limitations of autism made me question the things I had already done, what would they do to people just starting out? These limitations become self-fulfilling prophecies. They change what our children believe are possible, how they see themselves and the world. What if I became one more voice, one more reason that autistics and their families could ignore the predictions? I had the security of being self-employed, married, grown up. I had the privilege of a safe life that judgement wouldn't rock. More than that, I could make a difference. So, I decided to go public.

When I was diagnosed, I read the statistics. That scared me. I read the information, that saddened me. What resonated for me, what saved me, were the stories. The successes. Actually autistic. The frontline. People who live in the kind of parallel world that I see and feel, and who are figuring it out, too.

And this is who I am. Actually, it's who I always was, I just didn't know it. A lifetime lived as different, weird, alien, other. A certainty that I was weak and less-than. That I did not belong here. This is who I am.

And for the little ones coming behind me? If I self-identify, if I come out, I tell the world that being wired-up differently is okay, it's everywhere, it's sometimes even a superpower! And just as much, I tell myself.

As an adult, you get to decide what you focus on, what you create. Yes, you have to deal with the consequences of your past. Yes, you have to own the decisions you've made and the life you've had until now. But acknowledgement doesn't have to be an anchor. Free yourself. Accept that until now, you have been basing your life on bad data. You thought you were broken, damaged, oversensitive, and not good enough. You thought you were the problem. That ends now.

I always had a pull to explore my heritage. To understand why Māori language and art felt warm to me, like home. But the desire was gentle, easily delayed and distracted by work and life. So, I was a dabbler. A short course here, a book or event there. I wanted to know more, but there was a creeping shame that held me back. Who did I think I was? How dare I presume to be allowed in this space. Then I had kids. Suddenly, it was clear. They had no shame or hesitation around their place in the world, they had never heard of the blood quantum. Their world would be shaped by their experiences, and I could be part of that. If they grow up hearing the language, owning their identity, maybe I could heal and rewire in them what was disconnected in me. Maybe I could soften that shame for them. I could suck it up, be brave, take on the unknown to make it known for them. It's the whole theme of parenting, right? Sacrificing our own comfort and preferences so we can make the world better for our kids.

As an adult, I took the opportunity to create cultural connections. I wanted it for my children. But I was scared. Would I be told I wasn't 'Māori enough' the way I had been told at school? And what if I didn't feel the connection that I was hoping for? What if my own culture felt fake, pretend? It didn't matter, it couldn't. The only what if that really mattered was *What if I make a difference?*

One day, at a study session, I knelt next to a *kuia*, an older Māori woman. She was delicate with grey hair twisted with a bone clip, she had a *tā moko* (traditional Māori tattoo), and we were talking about why we were studying. She surprised me by saying she didn't speak the language. Her parents wanted her to be successful in a white world, so they only ever spoke to her in English. She was tearing up, I was tearing up. I explained that I wanted to be able to speak to my children in *te reo Māori* so they could be connected to their *whakapapa* (history). She nodded, and laughed '*āe, tautoko whanaunga mai*', and then, puzzled, she held her hand up against mine: 'So, how'd you get so white?'

I was stunned. She wasn't using my skin colour as proof I wasn't Māori, she was using my Māoriness as proof my skin wasn't right. She trusted what she knew with her heart, not what she saw with her eyes.

I thought if I learned to *kōrero Māori*, to speak the language of my ancestors, it would somehow make up for not having the right skin. But here she was with all the beauty, *mana*, and presence of what I considered a true Māori woman, and because she didn't speak the language, she didn't feel good enough. There are so many of us, disconnected from who we are, in so many ways. Ashamed because we don't 'look right', ashamed because we don't 'sound right', ashamed for not knowing what we don't know. I knew that she was Māori, not for what she could do or say, but for who she was. And maybe I could start to believe that was true for me, too.

As I continue my journey into my culture, my origin story, I am finding the connections. And not just through shared history, but also for a shared perspective, a way of seeing the world. For my fear of not belonging, of not being enough no matter how much I learn or grow. I feel my ancestry calling me to be whole, but how? I am full of shame for the places I am not enough: Am I this or that?

But what if my value is in being both? What if my journey *is* my place? *Āniwaniwa tū wae rua*, the legs of the rainbow stand in two different places. Let's consider this, the ability to walk between worlds: the indigenous and the colonizer, the autistic and the allistic, the seen and unseen. To survive I have had to find ways to soften the conflicts inside me. I have had to hold spaces that are both Māori and *Pākehā* (non-Māori), both introverted and extroverted, both diagnosed and undiagnosed, and all my other supposed contradictions. Holding these spaces, walking between worlds, lets me translate and interpret for others who are in the same spaces. My indigenous heritage and my neurodivergence lets me walk in many worlds – across cultures, across paradigms – without ever fully belonging. I have the honour of holding space and building bridges.

When you uncover your identity – cultural, neurological, magical – it means making choices about how you see yourself and how you see the world. It means letting go of the story you may have been told, so you can tell the story of the best you can be.

There is a spectrum, a kaleidoscope, and it's time to access the gifts of diversity. Diversity of brains, culture, skills, emotions. To seek the truths about who we are, and to see them as not only normal, but maybe even perfect.

During my Māori language study, I experienced my first traditional *marae* stay. Everyone in the class stays together in the *wharenui*, the huge open space meeting house. We bring sleeping bags, have meals together, and only speak in *te reo Māori* the entire time.

Even just being in the *wharenui* is special. The design of the building represents the human body, softly emanating ancestral wisdom. The diagonal bargeboards are carved arms and fingers welcoming you in, a ridge beam the spine, rafter ribs wrapped around the heart and spiritual centre of the space. Somehow, bringing our humanness into this sacred space – our breathing, our clothing, our technology – feels both grounding and uplifting.

On the first night, after a big day of learning, it was time to set up for bed. We all had blankets and sleeping bags, and everyone had to drag mattresses out to make our beds for the night. I froze. People everywhere, noise and social buzz, mattresses lined up like Tetris blocks and I couldn't move. A girl from my class caught my eye and I whispered, 'There's nowhere for me to sleep.' And it struck me, the feeling I'd had my whole life, that I had to fight for my place, that I didn't belong, I didn't fit. The girl laughed and said, 'I'll make a space for you.' The relief and the emptiness of it hit me all at once, how much it meant to me that she saw me as someone worthy of a space, someone to make a space for. And the sadness of my own need for that outside validation, to know that l am wanted, that l belong.

Imagine how it would be if Superman didn't know about his whole kryptonite issue, he's out at the supermarket one day and BAM! Kryptonite on Special! Embarrassing. Because you've built your life in layers, the meaning of a diagnosis can hit you in layers. A process of unlearning, unbecoming. l look back over my life now and see how much l fought reality. l pushed myself to learn to speak because l didn't know my physiology was working against me. l worked to pretend light and sound didn't bother me because l thought l was the only one. My sensitivity made me react differently to the people around me, but instead of easing into the world, l punished myself for not being enough. It never occurred to me that my differences were anything other than weaknesses to overcome. And as for being Māori? Well, Dad had told me my ancestors were Māori. But l still believed that to be Māori was something proven with actions and evidence, not a knowing in my bones.

> Intersectionality is a lens through which you can see where power comes and collides, where it interlocks and intersects.
> – Kimberlé Crenshaw[10]

Intersectionality acknowledges that the different aspects and identities of each person layer and combine to create different forms of privilege and discrimination, advantage and oppression. Every person has a unique experience in the world, and understanding this intersectionality, understanding our differences, is key.

Until you have a blocked nose, you hardly ever think to appreciate breathing freely. That's privilege. Not having an issue or need doesn't feel like an advantage, but it is. If you are neurotypical, you take for granted the many ways you are automatically accommodated in the current world. You have neurotypical privilege.

Storytelling around a flickering fire has given way to shimmering celluloid and ad-free-tv-marathons. With technology we now have the ability to connect with more stories, more voices, more cultures, more brains. Our role-modelling can come through media representation, but we need more stories from all voices, all cultures, all brains.

By sharing your story, you rewrite normal. You carve out a space for yourself and you make space behind you for others to follow. It's time for neurodivergents, for all people, to truly take on the idea that normal is what we decide, what we create. That our identities no longer have to conform into binary boxes.

Because we're part of an omniverse. A world where we are all. Not *one*, because we are not one. We are a billion. Incredible. Individual. Ones. We are not this *or* that, we are this *and* this *and* this *and* this. *Kotahi tonu te Wairua o nga mea katoa*, there is one Spirit that flows through all.

The lines between science and magic, nature and technology, technology and magic – it's all blurring, defined only by how we see things and what-we-see-as possibility. DNA and ultra-violet light revealed an entire world of new evidence, changing the way we look at crime scenes (and hotel rooms!). We don't know how much we can't see yet. So much of science can be magic, so what if magic is just science we haven't yet discovered?

Your existence, our existence, determines and rewrites normal. Ideas exist in a space where there is no time, just connection. Sometimes even literally! I can be in Aotearoa, New Zealand, at 6am, while you see me live from New York at 2pm, or virtually, online, or reading my words at any time – but in this moment of connection, we are one.

And what if it doesn't have to be binary? One or the other? What if we can have both? The diagnosis and the support, the identity and the understanding?

If there's something about yourself that you push down, ignore, hate, something that makes you different. Take a breath. Consider: What if your difference is your advantage? You can spend energy attacking your weaknesses or you can accept the ways they fit together to make you perfect.

Every individual has a specific, unique magic they bring to the world. Uncovering that truth about yourself will unlock your powers and unleash your super.

- ▶ An autistic with double passions for arcade games and entomology led to the creation of a magical empire. That's autistic Pokémon creator Satoshi Tajiri.

- ▶ An autistic turned her overwhelming environmental malaise into a global movement. That's Nobel-prize nominated autistic Greta Thunberg.

And it doesn't have to be big, personal-brand-defining stuff. It can be the everyday ways you connect cultures or ideas. For example, I can use my instincts as a parent to connect with other parents (that is, I am totally invested in getting the vegetables into the child). But I'm also autistic, so I totally understand that, from the autistic's point of view, there is a lot of food that is trying to kill us and must be avoided at all costs.

Blueprint Action: Bridges

You can use your energy to fit in, or use it to find and explore your niche. What worlds do you walk between?

What basic, binary ways do you label yourself and the people around you? Take those labels and try reframing them. How could you start seeing yourself in new ways?

What would help you create genuine authenticity?

Are there opportunities to reframe your challenges and squeeze out magic?

Listen to the part of you that is made of the same stuff as Shakespeare and stars. Quantum physics, right? You can see the crap in life, or you can see the cool. It's all there. Being able to choose what we focus on is a freedom we don't appreciate (or utilize) enough.

People now are multi-spectrum, kaleidoscopic. For so many of us, identity is a journey, and it is huge. We are being diagnosed as neurodivergent late, we are connecting with our culture as adults, we are choosing to shape our *whānau* going forward.

A jawbreaker is created with hundreds of layers of rock-hard candy. The creator starts with a single grain of sugar, adding liquid candy layers one by one. As each layer hardens another layer is added, using different colours and flavours to create a solid ball. Finished jawbreakers can include hundreds of layers, and the process can take weeks. As you suck, you dissolve the thin candy layers one by one until you reach the speck of candy at the centre.

Sit quietly, hold your breath. Even in stillness you are buzzing in a billion ways. All the swirling little cells that make up your heart, your brain, your lungs. And as your skin sheds, your hair grows, and your eyelashes fall, you change and evolve. Moment by moment, cell by cell.

There's just one thing about you that never changes. The speck of candy at your centre. That's the glow, the light that waits to be more of itself. The light that grows when you feel good. It sparkles when you're confident, it shimmers when you connect. The glow? It's who you really are. You are peaceful. You are magic. You feel good. The glow is you before you knew you were anything other than perfect. Because guess what? You are a jawbreaker! Thousands of layers of rock-hard candy, so strong that it appears to be a single delicious mouthful. From the outside you might look as though you are solid, total, real. You might appear to be a rubbery green. But underneath you are pearly blue, scratchy yellow, shiny red. You are a million moments. You have created yourself bit by bit and layer by layer, every day since you were born. *E mōhiotia ana a waho kei roto he ana*, one cannot know from the outside what is contained within.

Your beautiful sticky layers represent your life so far. They represent you, so far. But they are not you-right-now. You (right now) are a creator of layers. You are building your jawbreaker, bit by bit. You create layers with your choices, your thoughts, and your feelings. This exact moment is the outermost layer, the shell. Right now, you are melting candy layers with your mind. Tomorrow? Today's actions and decisions will be part of your jawbreaker. Little by little, big by big. What layers are you creating today?

But you know, dissolving your past doesn't mean forgetting it. It means honouring the ways that your past has built you and changed you, and then using it to move forward in the best ways for you. If there's something in your past that you want to dissolve, nuke it! Go to therapy, journal, or talk to friends. Speak up, speak out, or change your mind. Do what you need to do to feel okay. Then get clear: Yes, your life up until this point has made you who you are, but you don't have to wear it on a t-shirt. You can make the decision to be here and now.

Feel yourself at the edge of exactly who you are meant to be. Make today's layer as close to the glow at your centre as you can. Make it as happy, and peaceful and you, as you can. And most of all? Stop rolling around in old junk. Use your energy for moving towards what you want. (And if you don't know what you want? How about starting with what everyone wants – to feel good! While you figure out what your perfect world looks like, just focus on feeling good, free, and happy in your life.)

You know, it's okay to just bring the best of your past with you. It's okay to let go of the bad you've left behind. And it's okay to be fresh and now and you. All of your past – every path taken, every decision made, and every bit of learning you've done – has brought you to now. And now is what matters.

Of course, you might not want to change. Or you might not be ready to change yet. That's okay. This is for if and when you do. You're not ready yet? You don't have to be. Your world will be ready when you are.

Think of it this way. You create your life in layers by directing energy. This is a lot like money. You can spend it, and you can earn it. You can't spend the same dollar on both ice cream and books. So, you make a choice. Or you make more money. Same with energy. You can spend your energy creating, motivating, and allowing, or you can spend it whinging, whining, and boo-hooing. You usually can't do both at the same time! Make smart choices, create more delicious layers.

I'm not saying never spend any negative energy, do it! Take that nap, have that cry, that grizzling session, or that six-month pyjama party. Change the channel for yourself in a big way. Just make sure that you do it on purpose. Make it a choice, not a side effect. Make it work for you. If marinating in bad feelings helps you work through them, then do it. Sort things out as efficiently as you can, get help, then change your focus. And don't hang around in crap you can't change. Liquefy it and live now!

Your outer layer is the one you've worked for, the place you've been brought to. But if you decide you are ready for change, big change? Then make room. Stop. Throw it away. Cancel, resign, break up. Let the universe know that you are ready for what's next. Get ready for the yes. Because as you do, space will open up for exactly what you want.

Change is exciting. When you are willing to change, it means that you have the power to be different, to be yourself, and you do. Because there's only one thing keeping you in this place: a decision. A year from now you will have a new world, new layers, even a new body. Bit by bit, cell by cell. Thank the old pieces of you – they brought you here, then let them go. Choose your layers from here on out.

Every day you create layers. You learn something new, drop or grow habits, and make new connections. You create yourself layer by layer.

Think about who you are. How are you different from a day ago? A week ago? Or when you were five? What candy layers have you added? To get a clearer idea of where you are and how far you've come, let's get creative! You can create your jawbreaker as a story, or an image.

Blueprint Action: Your Jawbreaker

1. Start with the glow at the centre. The You. Your brand. This is who you really are, no matter what. It might be sparkly, mellow, or kick-ass. It might even be blank for now, waiting for inspiration! But whatever it is, it makes you feel good!

2. Create chronological layers. Special dates and events: your birthday, the arrival of a sibling, meeting a friend, any time that is significant for you.

3. Create logistical layers. When you started school or moved house. Layers of practical change.

4. Create biological layers. Have you ever broken a bone? Been sick or in hospital? Did you wear glasses or braces? Get a piercing?

5. Write people layers. The different people who came into or moved through your life. Friends, teachers, mentors, guides. (Even people you've never met like characters or celebrities can be important layers in your life!)

6. Create object or treasure layers. Your favourite toys, books, clothing, cars... anything you can touch that's special to you.

7. Create layers that represent choices. Choices that shaped your world. The new outfit, the friend, the essay topic, etc. Choices are valuable layers; they've led you to where you are!

8. Write emotional layers. Happy times, challenging times, things that you are proud or scared of. Emotional moments will often have strong feelings and memories attached to them.

9. Add virtue layers. Times that you were brave, times that you were kind or strong or creative.

Your life so far is a blend of all these layers (and more!). And you can add layers any time you like.

Jawbreaker tips:

▶ Make your layers different colours. You might make happy times yellow, or frustrating times purple.

▸ You could add symbols for memories of people or places or feelings. You might like to add photos or music.

▸ You don't have to include everything. Your jawbreaker doesn't have to be perfect or even complete. Your jaw-breaker represents how far you've come, and helps you understand who you are.

Once you have completed your jawbreaker, give it some time to marinate. Go for a walk, listen to some music, or set it aside for a few days. When you come back to it, you'll be able to admire how far you've come. That's when you can go to the very edge of your jawbreaker and create a thick new layer. This is the shell, this is the now. The now swirls with potential and choices. Picture yourself at the edge of your jawbreaker, using your energy today to create glittering new layers as perfect as the glow at the centre.

Autistics are not broken, we do not need to be fixed, and the only thing we suffer from is other people's ignorance. Some-times, we pick up on that ignorance as children and carry it with us.

I've spent my life working so hard to fix this feeling of wrongness, to blend in, be normal, be other-than-myself. What if acceptance is the cure? What if rather than studying and mimicking our atypical peers, we stay put? We say *Hi*? We hold our own? As deserving as any tree, beetle, or flawed human on the face of the earth. And as more of us are diagnosed, supported, acknowledged, it could mean permanent change. Lights dimmed in supermarkets. Tags removed from clothing. A quieter, calmer, world where neurodivergents are the majority. What if we stop aiming for sameness and embrace the complex, a time and space where an individual is more than a bundle of symptoms? What if we started by adding our own voice to the mix? What if I start with me?

As I mentioned before, *takiwātanga* is a Māori expression

for autism, it means in his or her own time and space, and how beautiful is that? As I continue my journey into *te ao Māori* (the Māori world), I see more and more that it is a universe. A lifelong journey. But also? It is innate. It is my birthright. I can learn and grow because I want to, because it is fun and hurts in good ways, but it is not compulsory. Being Māori, like being autistic, is a way of experiencing the world. And it is a way of being that I don't have to prove or earn, because it is who I am. No, I may never feel 'Māori enough' in the ways that my ego has invented. But I can feel steady in my own skin. And I can use that understanding. I can be another voice, another example, another possibility. I can be the role model I didn't have, and that is true no matter what I decide to do next.

And you? You grew up. You survived. You made it. And all the things that made you different then? Make you different now. They fit together perfectly. Believe it. You are the answer to someone else's question, you are the open door. Whether you share your story, or don't, you exist. And your existence rewrites normal.

Scene Nine

The New World

I can't go back to yesterday, because I was a different person then.

Lewis Carroll, *Alice's Adventures in Wonderland*

So, I'm lying on the hospital bed with my eyelids prised open like in *A Clockwork Orange*. I'm sedated but not unconscious, and even though I'm twenty-one years old and fully grown, the nurse has tucked a teddy bear in under my arm. I would laugh, but I'm scared, my heart is already pounding because the doctor said to watch the red dot, and if I move my eyes I could be accidentally blinded.

I'd worn glasses since I was fourteen and the school board started getting blurry. And even though I logically understood laser eye correction surgery, I had read everything, watched the informational video with the cartoon eyeballs, paid for the surgery, and hoped for the best – some part of me didn't really believe it. So, before the surgery, when they asked me to remove my glasses and leave them behind? I kept them. They were going to put a laser in my eyes, and (in most cases and if everything goes well) change my vision? It sounded futuristic. Magical. Unbelievable. And then I smelled something. Something very distinctive. They tell you the smell is 'perfectly normal, just the laser interacting with the air', but I knew better. They were burning my eyeballs.

Human beings are different in hundreds of ways, ways you can see, ways you can't. Some of us may appear to be more the same than others, but how things look isn't always how things are. When we uncover and acknowledge difference, we honour identity. We validate our reality.

As a child, I cried at night. A sadness with no source. A punishment, I thought, for being different. When I got older, I tried to talk to doctors, tried to explain the hole inside me. I was diagnosed with General Anxiety, Major Depressive Disorder. Autism? Was considered but dropped, they wrote things in my notes like 'no issues at school', 'makes jokes', 'smiles easily', and 'makes eye contact'. It wasn't the doctors' fault, they were looking for what they expected to see. They were looking for the classic signs of autism. But the diagnostic criteria for autism were developed by a Dr Dude, studying a Bunch of Boys.

So not only have we been defined and diagnosed against neurotypical, deficit-based standards, but autism has even been branded 'blue' – because researchers assumed it was a predominantly 'male' condition. Okay, so wait a minute, then what's with all the women being diagnosed now? What's with all the stats that show a strong correlation between neurodiversity and gender diversity? There is an incredibly strong cross-over between the autistic and rainbow community. So, hold on to your genitals, let's have a quick look at autism and gender!

No, autism doesn't have a gender. Surprise! But the current (aka racist, colonized, ableist) world has been built around two very strict, very straight (#SorryNotSorry) genders. A binary system where you are one or the other, a male or a female, based on your having or not having a penis. Simple systems aren't always accurate or inclusive. Meanwhile, gender and sexual diversity has been present in indigenous cultures since forever, acknowledged and honoured alongside neurodivergence as sacred gifts. Unfortunately, so much indigenous wisdom was scrubbed out and pushed down by beliefs centred on blanched, puritanical heteronormative misinformation. Fast-forward to now and we are stuck with this idea that a penis-having male in the old world looked a certain way, and acted a certain way. *Nō reira...*

When a male doesn't speak or make eye contact, we say: Hmmm, could be autistic.

When a female doesn't speak or make eye contact, we say: Aww, she's just shy.

When a male lines up his toys, we say: Hmmm, could be autistic.

When a female lines up her toys, we say: She's so neat and organized.

When a male is super-interested in trains, we say: Ha! Could be autistic!

When a female is super-interested in Barbies, we say: Wow, she just loves Barbies.

The same basic behaviours and intentions, but a completely different perspective based on what a colonized society expects and accepts from one of only two genders. And yay you if you're an autistic that ticks the current diagnostic criteria because gender isn't the only thing that can get in the way of diagnosis. Lots of us employ survival skills that can also really mess up the process. But no matter what genitals we're born with, or gender, sexuality, or expression we are, lots of us have talents in social mimicry, and mask our autistic traits so we don't fit beautifully into the current diagnostic criteria.

And there is a price for masking – shutdown, meltdown,

and long-term burnout. Here again, we bump up against the old world, the old world that tells us, 'The only feeling males can express freely is anger.'

So, while a male-identifying autistic might be melting down, yelling and breaking things in a classroom, the female-identifying autistic may be shutting down, unable to speak, or move. Because the old world says, 'Girls should be nice and good. Quiet and likeable.'

One kid is flipping desks, running, screaming. Woah! We can see there's a problem. Let's get this in a box, ASAP! Meanwhile, another kid is quiet, in a dark spot, under the radar, easy to miss.

Both kids reacting to overload, reacting to stress, but reacting in the ways that society has told them is acceptable. Does this mean females are less likely to be autistic, or just more likely to present differently? What about the trans kids? The nonbinary kids? And when you consider gender diversity, expression, and human individuality, does it even make sense to consider genitals at all?

Doctors can be amazing resources, but remember they're also just people, and they don't – and can't – know everything. Self-diagnosis is valid and accepted in the autistic community, because so much information about autism has not yet filtered into daily medical practice. If someone tells you they're autistic, believe them. Anyone who shares their identity deserves respect. They're certainly not doing it for the prestige, support, or understanding that society provides with it. Guys, autistics don't even get special car parks. (We should.)

It's important to talk to professionals who understand the different ways autism presents across people. And don't be put off if the first doctor you talk to doesn't get it. Keep going until someone hears you. Researchers have confirmed that the diagnostic process is flawed for women, girls, and gender-diverse *any*one. What they're working on now is how to best diagnose, and importantly, support, all autistics. Bottom-line? This is not a find-it-and-fix-it situation. This is revolution, the flipping of cultural norms, and does it surprise me that gender-diverse people are (according to current research) six times more likely to be autistic or neurodivergent than their peers? No! That's like saying, 'Research shows that awesome people are even more awesome, more sensitive, more conscious, and more designed to shape a new world.' Yeah, I'm not surprised at all.

- ▶ Both experience feelings of being in the wrong body, or on the wrong planet.

- ▶ Both can be alienated from their biological families.

- ▶ Both feel the pull of pretending to be a certain way ('normal', *shudder*) to be accepted.

- ▶ Both can feel isolated and rejected, with sky-high suicide rates and time in the mental health system.

If you've got a feeling about your body, or your brain, you are not alone. Be brave. Keep looking, find the professional who gets you. It's like any relationship, it might take a few tries to get right! But I promise, once you find it, professional support, and greater understanding of who you are unlocks the next level.

We've talked about the glow at the centre of your jawbreaker, the part of you that is most *you*. The you that feels happy, confident, and at peace. Well, it's time to snuggle up! Because even though that glow is at the centre of you, and might only be a tiny spark right now, you can stoke it, grow it, and make it as big as you want!

The first time I felt the glow, I was a teenager, and I was in a very dark place. I was sad, sadder than I could express or understand, and in my darkness I felt completely alone. I cried a lot, I wrote a lot, and one day, in the worst of it, I realized there was something with me in the dark. A speck, a spark, a glowing brightness – something that even my sadness couldn't touch.

It wasn't enough to get me out of the darkness on its own, but it was hope. The glow was the beginning of my understanding that we all have something inside us that's completely special, irreplaceable, and stronger than we know.

While I didn't jump straight into the glow after that, I did start to notice it. I noticed that it sparkled when I read books I loved, it quivered when I was around rainbow colours and Christmas decorations, it swelled when I went to the movies, and it sparked and exploded when I was writing. In moments when I felt connected to something good and pure about me, it was like the glow was bigger than I was – pulling me to be even more of my best self.

When you feel the glow, you are exactly who and where you are meant to be. It's the delicious warm feeling at the centre of your jawbreaker, that peaceful fizzy aura of confidence that you get when you feel good, and you know that you're doing the right thing for you.

When you get into your glow, you're connected with the best part of yourself. Think of your glow as being any feeling that registers as good. From this place, you will feel happier and more confident, make better decisions, be kinder to yourself, and know more clearly what you want! You feel good – whatever that means for you. It could be peaceful, happy, fizzing, alive, excited, motivated, inspired, or it could be a combination! A swirling mix of awesomeness!

Blueprint Action: The Glow

Finding ways to connect with your glow can give you speedy access to some of your greatest tools, so let's do it!

For me, accessing the glow is all about fireworks! That means: Finding the fuse, Feeling the fuse, Feeding the fuse, Firing the fuse.

Finding the fuse

The fuse is the part of you that expresses your glow, it's where it comes from and where it lives, the feeling in your body. (Like the opposite of a nyeugh!) The fuse is the beginning.

To find the fuse start picturing something you love. Try thinking about your favourite food or music, and notice how your body reacts. Is there a change? For some people, it's a pounding (or fluttering!) heart, for others it's a light head, goose bumps or a perma-grin, kicky feet or tingly fingers – or it might even be all six!

Start thinking about all the things you love. Make a list. And get really specific. Try to pin point exactly what it is about that activity, person, or thing that makes you go gooey. For example:

> *I love movies.* I love it when the music swells during trailers, the way pieces of me fall away as I connect to the other hearts and brains watching alongside me. When the lights go down my heart pounds and I feel myself disappear into the screen, and for me that's amazing!

> *I love writing.* I love the way words bubble up in my brain, and spill out onto paper. I love translating information into bite-sized chunks, so readers can connect with it. Ooh, or creating something from scratch! Empowering people with ideas! When I write I feel powerful and connected, even in my pyjamas!

Feeling the fuse

Once you have found your fuse, settle in and observe it. How does it feel? Light and bubbly? Cuddly and cool? Does it have a texture? Feathery? Smooth? Or radiate a colour?

It might even have a taste or a smell! Get in and really feel it! Do this by picturing something that would be exciting for you (achieving a goal, winning a race, cracking open a new book – anything!). Then just pay attention... The glow could kick off with a tightening in your belly, a big grin, bright red sparks in your mind, it might even feel almost like fear at first, because of the intense feelings and adrenalin rushing through you.

Soon, we'll look at how to change what the glow feels like, but for now just find that fuse and notice exactly what it feels like for you in this moment.

Feeding the fuse

Like any feeling, you can grow your glow by feeding it! The simplest way to feed a feeling is to give it lots and lots of attention. Feel it as often as you can, as you drift off to sleep at night, when you wake up in the morning, in the shower or on the train, whenever you have a moment to tune in and feel good! Just feeling and admiring your glow will make it bigger and easier to access. With practice, you'll be able to connect anywhere, anytime! (We'll look at some more ways to connect at the end of this scene!)

Firing the fuse

Being able to set it off when you want to is super handy! In Neuro Linguistic Programming* there is a tool called *anchoring*. Anchoring is when you connect (or anchor) a very specific feeling to an object, action, or sensation. Lots of autistics do this instinctively.

For example: Is there a song that reminds you of

---

*   Neuro Linguistic Programming is the study of communication and human behaviour, how we interpret language to design our lives. I love learning about how the brain works and how we can use it to make our world more fun and effective!

summer? A necklace or shirt that makes you feel good when you wear it? (You can have anchors to sad or negative feelings, too, but we'll focus on the good ones!)

You're creating anchors all the time, just by living your life and connecting feelings to the things in your environment. The trick is to start creating them on purpose! To set an anchor:

1. Pick a feeling. This feeling could be confidence, calm, excitement. Or, like we've been talking about, it could be the absolute best feeling of being you – your glow!

2. Create the feeling. As strong as you can. This is where you get to decide how you want your glow to feel. Tweak it, describe it, feel it as intensely as you can and then...

3. At the peak of the feeling, touch the object/listen to the music/perform the activity/smell the smell. This is the moment you connect (or anchor) the feeling.

4. Repeat! The more often you do it, the stronger the anchor will become.

Then, when you need a boost, you can trigger the anchor. Put the music on and see if your glow follows, hold the object and tune into the feeling. Use the anchor to trigger the feeling, and use the feeling to strengthen the anchor. The more you do it, the stronger and easier the connection to the feeling will be.

Here are some more ideas for connecting to your glow:

▶ Did you ever have a special toy or book? Something that

when you held it, you felt happy and whole? That item could be connected to your glow.

▶ You might be able to express your glow through art: paint it, draw it, sculpt it, Photoshop it! Make it digital and use it as your wallpaper, create a design and print it on a t-shirt. Post it everywhere!

▶ Create a playlist of your absolute favourite, take-over-the-world, can't-get-them-out-of-your-head, just-got-to-jump-around-your-lounge-dancing songs. To make them extra effective, play them whenever you feel amazing. That way, you reinforce all the good feelings, and if you need to use them to feel better they are recharged with fresh positivity!

▶ If you know you're heading out to have a particularly awesome day, pick your clothing carefully! Take the opportunity to connect your glow to clothing, shoes, and accessories, too!

Remember: you don't need anything physical to connect to your glow. It can be as simple as closing your eyes, or clicking your fingers! Your glow is a feeling that you have inside of you; it's a part of you always! These ideas are just some ways you can access your glow even more quickly and easily.

Have you seen the meme showing grass under a microscope? It turns out that if you zoom in on the cells of some kinds of grass, you can see tiny faces. Smiles beaming up out of the green. Imagine – there are things that literally *make your cells smile*. I reckon I get this with perfect combinations – of light, sound, colours, words, and textures. Do you know some things that make your cells smile? Music? Space? Peace? Access your glow, and you can shine from the inside, starting now!

When you act from that pure, passionate light inside your-self, you change the world. You are expressing your unique gifts and talents. Suddenly you're not just getting stuff, you're growing the glow. The glow becomes more of itself and you become more of who you're meant to be. It comes from your heart, not your head. You were born to be great – everyone is. No accidents, no coincidences – it's all for you.

You might hear about being 'authentically autistic'. It sounds good, but many of us don't know what it's like to be authentically autistic because it is not something we have been allowed to be. We may not have been given therapies or attempts to force us to fit in – but perhaps even more insidiously, we have learned to do it to ourselves.

So, we have to find each other. We have to see other autistics in the wild, successful, happy, thriving. Autistics can struggle in the neurotypical world, but often we light up around each other. We get to be ourselves and to know, really know, that we are not broken normal people, rather, perfect autistic people. Autistics have a shared sense of self that reaches across genders, ages, skills, and personalities. To be autistic is to be part of a culture. A rich and vibrant culture that shines with distinctive language, food, art, traditions, routines, and rituals. When we spend time with other autistics, our weirdness is suddenly normal, our awkwardness, confidence.

In my regular life, I have people who get (most of) my jokes. I'm publicly autistic now, so don't have to mask as much as some. I'm married, self-employed, with a home and a formal diagnosis; privileged in so many ways. But that's the thing: if you've never had a community, how can you know what you're missing?

When I was diagnosed, I didn't think to connect with others. I guess I was so used to feeling alone that it still didn't occur to me that I no longer was. When I first started spending time with other adult autistics in online groups, I was struck by our similarities. Sensory sensitivities? Snap! Tales of rejection? Snap! Societal discord? Snap! It was threads of resilience built over a lifetime of being an outsider. We were different individuals from the same tribe.

For people known for their social awkwardness, there's something decidedly cool about groups of autistics. It's the little things. It's people who laugh at your jokes. Who nod. Who get it. People who hold space for you with kind eyes before they even know you.

The Austistic culture is rising as we do, bubbling with sub-tribes (the grounded, the excitable, the technical, the artistic etc.) and woven together with an absolute knowing. You know, like gaydar but for autism. The Autistic culture features a unique way of being; and now, thanks to an online world that no longer depends on physical contact or sensory *anything*, autistics are finding community with other autistics. We are connecting, joining forces. Autistics are sharing experiences, advice, jokes. And it turns out, our social skills are not non-existent, they are *autistic*.

Here's where we talk about double empathy. Double empathy is the theory that a mismatch between two people can lead to faulty communication. Theory of mind? Empathy deficits? Out the window! Thanks to (autistic) Dr Damian Milton, who proposed that it's not only autistics needing to sharpen their skills. Communication goes both ways! As Dr Milton says: 'Individuals who have different ways of processing and experiencing the world will also have differing norms and expectations and would therefore find it difficult to empathise with each other.'[11]

So, autistic social skills, not no social skills. Autistics have social skills with other autistics. Until now, the focus has been teaching autistics to speak neurotypical, to be more like the majority. Make more eye contact, learn how to make small talk, tell white lies, understand weird neurotypical phrases like 'let's jump in the car'. Autistics speak autistic, neurotypicals speak neurotypical. These are two different cultures, two communication styles, two languages that need to be translated and understood. We don't need to change ourselves to fit in, we need support to navigate a world that (currently) is not designed for us.

What would it look like if we started thinking of autism as a cultural difference rather than a strictly neurological difference? As an entire culture of people plunged into an unfamiliar environment. What if we started to see the things we call 'neurodivergent supports and strategies' (e.g. pastoral care, mentoring, language changes, scheduling and timetable support, etc.) as more of a cultural navigation? This instantly boosts the respect, the nuances, the care that goes into supports. Because suddenly, you are not fixing a problem, you are adjusting a lifestyle. This increases trust and connection – it makes support strategies human strategies.

For autistics, spending time with other autistics can mean seeing our authentic selves, and the possibilities for our authentic selves, reflected back to us. It means feeling free to speak, behave, and think in ways we've been told, and believed, aren't okay. Our conversations bounce from the practical to the absurd, the sombre to the hilarious – and everywhere in between. In fact, I think the only thing autistics tend not to do is small talk. (Classic autistic communication!) The same way that autistics know we're different – in the playground, in the office, in the streets – is the way that when we are together, we know we are the same.

And no, it's not perfect. Like any community, we are made up of individuals – we have different experiences, ideas, opinions. We rub each other the wrong way (not literally), we have different strengths and weaknesses, different preferences and personalities, plenty of opportunities to disagree, and you know what that means? That means we're human. Surprise! Human. Not perfect, but not *wrong*. We're individuals, but we are the same where it counts and we know it. Respect and equality doesn't require a neurotype.

People say, 'I don't want the label!' But you know what? I

want the identity, the self-awareness, the understanding. The potential to feel okay in the world. A label – a diagnosis – is not a prediction. It just lights up what was always true. Language is the beginning of changing the way we see. Language is our filter, our focus. Everything is changing, and it's the neurodivergents with our blended senses and sensitivities who are going to make it happen – not with loud voices or by demanding, but through quietly carving our own paths and doing things in exactly our own way.

Because it's not about fitting in any more. It's about making the world your own. Every day, autistics are being diagnosed, are self-diagnosing, are realizing and sharing their identity, they are re-evaluating their priorities. It's time to honour our sensitivities, to acknowledge our needs and be okay with being who we are. No excuses, no apologies. The biggest lesson from the Autistic culture is that we can all experience the world differently. And that we have all of the power, and all of the responsibility.

Yeah, many adult autistics arrive late to the 'authentically autistic' party. And not just because we (typically) avoid parties. So now, after a lifetime of training ourselves to fit in, pretending the world doesn't hurt, and generally camouflaging as normal, how do we learn to be ourselves? By knowing there's nothing to learn at all.

So, I'm lying there on the hospital bed, watching the red dot, holding as still as my pounding heart and fear of possible blindness will allow, and yip, I could smell them – my eyeballs burning.

When the bandages came off, my eyes were blurry, my surroundings confused. I blinked to clear the blurriness. The eye chart across the room came into focus. I could see. One tweak, one zap, one scientific breakthrough, and... I. Could. See. It hit me in waves over the following weeks, the details of the world

– fine print, freckles, my toes in the shower, leaves on trees, big screen movies without fogged-up glasses – the details of the world, the billion tiny things that were always there but that I. Couldn't. See.

It's time to set aside your old eyes, blink away the blurriness, open yourself to a new vision of the world. To value difference. To see others – and yourself – as multi-layered, perfectly imperfect, intense, and incredible individual human beings. You deserve to be here, not because of what you do, or say, or have. You deserve to be here because you were born.

Autistic World Domination

We've been getting to know one of the best people on the planet – you! Being autistic isn't a choice, but knowing and accepting who you are absolutely can be. Autistic world domination means understanding who you are and designing a world that works for you.

I remember playing computer games as a kid. Tucked up in blankets, the satisfying clink of collecting points. The lights, the graphics. I played through mealtimes, through sleep, I went on digital adventures, felt the crush of defeat, and fought my way back, determined to play again.

Did you know you can only play Pac-Man for two hundred and fifty-six levels? And then the Pac-Man kill screen cuts you off – the game ends. But what if it didn't? Two fifty-seven is what happens when we go beyond what we can see, beyond what we think we know. Into the possibilities. The next level. Autism is a neurodivergency. Part of the new world. A world that is more sensitive, more conscious, more aware. Level two fifty-seven.

Wait up then, so what's up with our limited life span? If autistics are so clever, so magical, so sensitive, so awesome, and soooo next level, why is the average life span of an autistic person only thirty-six years? The research says autistics die sooner and develop more stress-related issues. We are under-employed – despite equal skills and qualifications – and we are overrepresented in the justice system – despite innate propensi-ties for honesty, rule-following, and fairness. Our life span is cut short because of a world that favours conformity, dishonesty, denial. We get stressed, sick, and traumatized by environments that demand we ignore our senses and fight our instincts. While neurotypical 'autism experts' scratch their heads, there is no mystery to most autistics that the second leading cause of death in our people is suicide. A deliberate, conscious choice to leave a hostile world. A world where who we are is seen as an abnor-mality in need of a cure.

If you are autistic, you are not broken. You do not need to be cured, fixed, changed, or trained. Fact: Autistics are better, faster, smarter. We spoke binary before computers. We were hands-free before Bluetooth. We don't waste energy with office politics, social games, or low-stakes claptrap.

Nearly 70 per cent of human beings are neurodivergent. Sensitive, truth-telling, innovative, powerful. And that number is growing. Because this is not an epidemic, this is a revolution.

I'm tucked up in the dark, flashing graphics, pumping soundtrack, I'm completing challenges, passing levels, collecting goodies. Imagine if we played life the way we played games? With a sense of joy? Gamification is about making life fun and rewarding, finding ways to feel good, to make our energy and our environment work for us. Is it a break-down or break-through? Limiting diagnosis or empowering identity? It's all in how we frame, or reframe, it.

In *te ao Māori*, the Māori world, *taniwha* roam the earth. Ancient monsters. These supernatural guardians, are powerful, mischievous, volatile; they guard waterways, and protect the natural world. Stories of *taniwha* connect people to their history and identity. They are referenced in indigenous songs, stories, *whakataukī* (sayings), they're used to explain natural phenomena and events, and to hold and pass knowledge down through the generations.

In 2002, the *Ngāti Naho hapū* (indigenous people) in the Waikato of Aotearoa, New Zealand,* objected to a highway being built that would destroy the lair of *Karu-Tahi*, the one-eyed *taniwha*. Controversy erupted, protests continued, and, eventually, government authorities agreed to partially reroute the highway.

Two years later, following the completion of the highway, there was some particularly bad weather and the Waikato River flooded. This flood destroyed the original path of the highway. But because the path had been moved, because of the calls of indigenous people to respect the *taniwha*, the rerouted highway was safe.[12]

Even among Māori, there is disagreement on the existence, relevance, and significance of *taniwha*. But what if, in ancient times, a strange weather pattern or epic storm event was wrapped up in the story of a *taniwha*? What if these fireside tales were passed down as cautions and advice about specific locations? And when threatened by colonization, how does a culture hold on to intergenerational knowledge? Through our DNA, through our stories. Like a nyeugh, a *taniwha* is a message. In *te reo Māori*, we say '*Patua te taniwha koi tamariki*', Kill the *taniwha* while it is young. Your world is sending you messages. Through your body, and your environment. Tune in and take action. Blending ancient wisdom with modern innovation is how we can discover and utilize the best of both worlds.

The average life span of an autistic person is thirty-six years. Half that of the average population. Autistics feel harder, think deeper, burn brighter, and die sooner. We tell neurotypicals to

---

* I am humbled and grateful for the permission and blessing of *Ngāti Naho* to share their story of indigenous guardianship.

'just do it', 'carpe diem' – well they've got time to waste. Your days are limited. Your minutes are precious. Taking action this second brings you closer to your dreams, and doing nothing lets them drift further away.

You've made the decision that you're worth it. You've read through this book and now have tools, ideas, and maybe even a total blueprint for world domination. A plan that is utterly yours, to create a world that will be perfect for you. And although it is finished for today, it's a work in progress. Because now that you have dreamed and stretched, and allowed yourself to aim for the greatest of all possible worlds, there's a new path ahead.

It's time to let go of your beautiful plans, and detailed goals. Have faith that when you are open, the life planned for you is greater than anything you could draw up. Now? You might follow your blueprint exactly, or sculpt it as you go, but either way you've told the universe that you want more. You want more happiness, success, peace, love, joy. You want more you! You want world domination!

You control the choices you make, the actions you take, and the life you get. And as you do it, you can show others they can do the same. Look at how far you've already come:

Scene One: Neurodiversity Is the Key

You learned that you are not alone! You set the foundation. You got inspired. You decided to ask for what you want, and to be the hero of your story. You chose to put on your cape and your red shirt. (And sometimes, your brown pants!)

Scene Two: World Domination

You started hunting down your dreams. You identified the things that make your heart pound, and you found ways to pull them into your life. You defined and designed the ultimate world for you.

Scene Three: Reframe and Target

You explored empowering language. You created SMART goals to set your heart pumping. You lined up your perfect world, knowing that everything is possible for you!

Scene Four: Sensitivity Is Power

You identified your challenges. You started digging for more of the truth about you. You uncovered more ways to take charge of your world, and you learned how your sensitivities give you power.

Scene Five: Human Mercury

You analysed the way you read and respond to the environment, and found ways to respect and replenish your energy. You got it on paper. Step by step. Bit by bit. You carved out a direct path to your dreams. You created a plan, now prepare to launch!

Scene Six: Energy and Fire

You learned how you spend energy with your words, your actions, and decisions. As you follow through on your plans, you now know that everything you do makes a difference to the world. You don't have to be rich or famous (or anything else!) to transform the planet. You're doing it now.

Scene Seven: Autism-Friendly Is Human-Friendly

You saw how neurodivergent-friendly spaces are growing. You found support, advice, and people to share your success with. You recruited an army for world domination. And you found ways to get to the yes!

Scene Eight: The Bridge Builders

You learned how the worlds you walk in, and the ways that you are different, work together to make you perfect. Your uniqueness makes your significance on the planet unmistakable. You realized that your value is in being exactly who you are.

Scene Nine: The New World

You looked for more ways to learn about yourself and your world. You made the move from binary to spectrum, embracing multi-layered words and ways of being. You figured out your strengths. What do you love? What are you good at, what lights you up? That's where you belong.

Splashed across your blueprint are your pounding heart and glowing brain. This is the plan that you can follow for as long as it feels good to you. By pushing and challenging yourself, you have opened up to the ultimate possibilities, so it's time to relax.

Blueprint Action: Let Go

Wait, what if things go wrong? What if your plans crumble, your progress falters, you change your mind? What if the path goes dark? What if the process of taking over your world is just So. Painfully. Slow? That is the reason for this scene. You set your intentions, you make your plans, and then you *let go*. You get out of the way. You detach from the outcomes and give yourself the gift of freedom. Because as much as it feels good to take charge, and to know exactly what is happening and when, it can also be a lot of responsibility and a lot of work. So, this is you standing back and saying, 'Everything in its own time, in its own space. Everything will work out in the best ways for me.' When you let go, you trust that forces bigger than you (God, the universe, science, serendipity, sugar) will carry you. You allow your path to be carved without effort or desire. You can breathe. You can let your life be blue sky with cloud dreams that come and go. That feeling of peace comes with knowing you belong here. That the planet is a better place with you on it. And it is.

Give yourself the freedom to change your mind. Be flexible. Don't get so set in your plans that when the world offers you other opportunities, you turn them away. As you go along you may discover different worlds, or open up new dreams. People leave medical school to become monks; they swap scholarships for gap years or live at home to care for their parents... People give up an old dream for a new one. That's your choice as ruler of your world. Your happy ending changes all the time – let it! You are a creator, a world builder, and you are ready for anything.

You can take action this day, this minute, this *second*, that will lead directly to whatever you want in your world. Now is just the beginning! You can prove it on paper, and you can kick it off today!

So, know this: Your life is in the moment, and the time to enjoy it is now. Play, have fun, find ways to make yourself happy. This is your life, and the world is yours. Any way you want it to be.

A special note for anyone who feels stuck in the wrong place, the wrong family, or the wrong job: Feel like you don't belong? Like you stick out? What if the reason you stick out isn't bad? What if all the things that you hate yourself for being when you're there are your strengths? And you're wasting them because you don't want to fail at fitting in to a place that sucks?

Feel good because you've been brave, because you've stuck it out, and you've made it this far. Feel good because you've reached a place where you're ready to make a move. You're in the place where you want to go, more than you care where. And that's when you get to decide. Know now that the real world is not the one they tell you. The real world is the one you wrap yourself up in. The one you create.

Because every weakness is a strength in the right environment. In a family of lawyers, the criminal is the black sheep. But in a family of criminals, it's the lawyer who's a disappointment! Different doesn't mean less. And autistic challenges, more often than not, come from a world designed for average, but our strengths? Our strengths can be superpowers!

If you know an autistic, love an autistic, or are an autistic, the time is *now*. Stop 'getting by', stop 'making do', stop 'waiting until'. You have everything you need. You are ready. You were born ready. Be in the world, on fire now. Burning with who you are and what you're here to do. It's worth repeating: If you are autistic, you are not broken. You do not need to be fixed. Not happy? Leave. Not appreciated? Feeling nyeugh? Go. Don't wait to find places and people who get you. Shine. And they will find you.

There is a place where you belong, where your strengths are strengths, where inclusions aren't inconveniences, where you will be appreciated. Keep looking and keep the faith! And while you're at it? Work on some grey thinking: it's not all or nothing. You can keep your day job (for now!) and write your screenplay at night. You can get through a day at work to get to your after-hours project. You can work from home, you can talk to employers. You can create your dream world bit by bit. You don't have to know exactly what you're doing or where you're going – just follow what feels good.

Autistics? Assemble! Your identity is yours, to share only when (and if) you want to. And meanwhile, wear the soft clothes. Stim. Sign. Speak. Or don't. Do what you need to do to feel right in this world. Autistic world domination means autistics having the same confidence, independence, and respect as every other neurotype.

And best of all, enjoy the way your senses let you experience joy! Autistic joy can be specific to each individual, so it's okay to feel unsure. Don't try to define it. The point is to look for it. Fine tune your senses and find the power in your unique autistic joy. What gives you goosebumps? What brings you completely into the present moment? Allow it. Feed it and breathe into it.

This is the new world, a world where there aren't tags in clothes, and where people will say, 'Your kid's not autistic? Not special? Oh, I'm so sorry! Aren't you worried they'll never work?'

Now, you will let go of your beautiful plans and detailed goals. You will relax, have faith, and know that you are open to the ultimate possibilities. More than ever before we live in a world where anything (everything!) is possible. Your blueprint will get you exactly what you want, and you will change the world. You have one life, one shot, and all the power to make it happen. Think big! Be you! Design and dominate – your world is ready when you are!

Welcome to Autism. The next level. Autistic world domination means you can be, do, or have anything. Your existence rewrites normal, and quietly, loudly, from the rooftops or to yourself, the autistic revolution is now!

Sample Blueprints

Your blueprint can look, feel, and be however you decide. An image, a poster, a poem, a diagram, a technical document, or a journal. As long as it inspires and motivates you! In this section, you'll find some sample blueprints.

Sample Blueprint Collage

Sample Blueprint Hand-drawn

Sample Blueprint Diagram-focused
Finishing my course

I want to finish my course. Be ready for the next phase of my life.

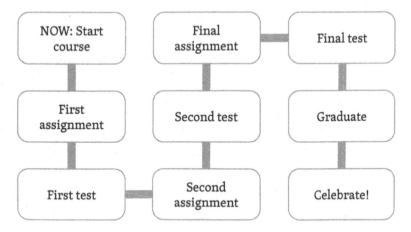

FUTURE: Finish course → complete internship → write resume → apply for jobs → get job

	MORNING	AFTERNOON	EVENING
MON	Volunteer work	Volunteer work	Study
TUES	Course	Course	OPEN
WED	Course	Study	Study
THURS	Study	OPEN	Online
FRI	Course	Washing and week prep	OPEN
SAT	Hiking or climbing	Reading	Reading
SUN	Sleep catch up	Online	OPEN

WEEK ☑ ☑ ☑ ☐ ☐ ☐ ☐ ☐ ☐ ☐ ☐ ☐ ☐ ☐ ☐

Energy in: Reading, time online, study, planning.
Energy out: Course days, exercise, people.

Sample Blueprint Sensory Style
Coping with sensory overwhelm

I like consistency and familiarity. I need strategies to cope with overwhelm.

- **Auditory**: I seem to notice sounds more than others. Music playlist and headphones, noise-cancelling headphones. I avoid busy, noisy, places (grocery shop online) or block out the sound with headphones.

- **Visual**: Safe space (e.g. I like to sit with my back to a wall), sunset lights, posters, decluttering to minimize overwhelm, create obvious places for important items.

- **Tactile**: Personal space, squeeze ball, poppers, putty, velvet piece, lip balm.

- **Smell/taste**: I like to smell peppermint and vanilla flavours. I chew gum to keep from biting pens (and the skin on my fingers!) and use an electric toothbrush.

- **Proprioception**: Heavy blanket, lap pad, balance board, stretchy bands.

- **Interoception**: Set reminders for regular infinity breathing and check my heart rate.

- **Vestibular**: Swinging/swaying, hanging upside down, trampolining and climbing.

- **Thermoception**: Sunblock reminders, check thermometer/weather forecast and make sure I feel comfortable as much as possible.

- **Alexithymia**: Journaling, and therapy. Maybe some art classes?

← Seeking . . . . Avoiding →

I want to start incorporating more sensory tools into my everyday life. These are as important to my body as food or medicine, and I'm going to be open to trying new things and learning about what works for me.

WEEKDAY SENSORY PLAN

	TASKS	TOOLS
6am	Wake up.	Phone alarm, peppermint oil, journal, meditation.
Breakfast	Prepare, eat, clean up.	White wide bowl, medium spoon, small spoon. Cereal, sugar, milk.
Ready for the Day	Shower, dressed.	Shower playlist, fan heater, soap, deodorant, lotion, fluffy towel, hair towel.
Transition to Work	Check slow cooker. Check schedule & diary. Leave house, bring bag, wallet, phone, headphones. Walk to bus stop.	Whiteboard checklist. Timer on slow cooker. Hooks for keys and bag station.
Work	Meetings, computer time. Challenges: interruptions, distractions, communication.	Headphones, notebooks & pens, fidgets, email templates, mentor to run messages by. Ask for written instructions.
Snacks and Meal	Snack: toasted sandwich, quiet time. Lunch (dinner leftovers). Snack: chocolate cake, quiet time.	Quiet room, bean bag, lap pad, sand art, headphones, morning/afternoon playlist. Quiet room, treadmill, squish balls.

cont.

	TASKS	TOOLS
Transition to Home	Check itinerary, catch bus, walk home. Get changed into home clothes.	Headphones, map and checklist, bus pass.
Dinner	Clean whiteboard checklist. Prepare dinner.	Cleaning wipes, kitchen utensils and gear, groceries. Music system.
After Dinner	Clean up, layout and prep for next dinner. Pack lunch for tomorrow.	Schedules and to-do lists. Food containers.
Prep for Tomorrow	Clothes ready, bag packed, wallet ready, phone on charge. Friday: Online grocery shop.	Lists, hangers ordered, multiple chargers. Grocery favourites list.
Bedtime	Routine to fall asleep.	Vanilla oil, journal, meditation, science audiobook, silky pillow.

WEEKEND SENSORY PLAN

	TASKS	TOOLS
TRANSITION TO WEEKEND	Grocery delivered and unpacked. Friday night roast dinner & TV show.	Online shopping.
Recovery	Recovery sleep.	Weighted blankets, guided meditation audio.
Play (optional)	Trampolining, indoor wall climbing.	Indoor adventure park passes, hoodies.
Ready for Next Week	Washing. Food prep.	Washing organizing chart, music playlist.
TRANSITION TO THE WEEK	Sunday night pasta dinner & TV show.	Food & crunchy snacks.

NOTES: Looking at this schedule now, I don't think it's sustainable long term. I don't have a lot of time just for me, and when I do schedule it in, I usually end up sleeping or doing stuff around the house. I can see how much of my time is spent either preparing to handle stress or recovering from handling stress. I can also see that I need heaps of recovery time each day and over the weekend. I want to have more energy available for myself, for joy (or at least fun?!), but still keep my income level up.

→ To do this, I'm going to: talk to my boss about remote work, and either trial that, or if they aren't open to it, start looking for a work from home role that will let me decrease energy going out.

Sample Blueprint Text-based

Scene One: Neurodiversity Is the Key

I'm good with numbers, I like cats, I have nice eyes, I like every kind of pasta with cheese sauce only, I want to have a small group of friends, I want to have regular alone time, I like to watch TV shows on repeat, I like to mountain bike, I want to join a local gaming group.

I want to feel like I belong and still be myself.

Scene Two: World Domination

Stress around people, stress around emotion and conflict, setting boundaries.

Flight is my main defence, my heart pounds, I feel sick, I leave as soon as I can. As a kid, I had a lot more meltdowns, but I still feel the pressure building sometimes and need to get to a safe space.

I think maybe I also shut down but I just thought I was lazy and useless.

Now I know that I need time away from people to recharge.

Relax: My safe place is my room. I keep it dark and have a galaxy light, lots of blankets, gaming. I like my sound loud so use headphones a lot of the time. I've been getting a good feeling from mountain biking lately, so I want to make that a more regular thing.

🌑 🌓 🌕 Scene Three: Reframe and Target

Be: I want to feel comfortable and confident.

Do: I want to make a small group of friends. SMART: Meet regularly in real life with a small group of friends who share a common interest over the next year.

Have: I want to have a bigger gaming system and a new bike. More of the hoodies that I like.

I've been called: shut off, robotic, quiet, shy, awkward, rigid.

I could reframe them as: objective,
consistent, individual, certain.

🌑 🌓 🌕 Scene Four: Sensitivity Is Power

Fears/Hates: I hate shopping, I have materials I prefer. Things have to feel right. I like sound to be balanced, and the things around me to be neat and organized. People say I walk funny but I don't know what that means. I like biking because I don't think about how my body looks so much. I don't like many different foods, but I don't care, I like what I like. I have trouble reading other people's emotions and expressing mine, but it only bothers me when other people get grumpy about it.

BE DO HAVE

BE: I want to feel comfortable and confident. I want to be a good listener and a good team member.

→ As long as I am trying and learning, I am successful. Every no is one closer to the yes.

DO: I want to make a small group of friends. I'm worried I won't fit in. I'm scared I'll always be weird.

→ When I find the right people, I will be weird with them :)

HAVE: I want to have a bigger gaming system and a new bike. More of the hoodies that I like.

→ I get anxious biking on public roads, my thoughts race and I start sweating. It's a brain fear and I want to work on it. → I can look for an alternative route. If I can't find an alternative route, I can take defensive driving lessons. I can get more safety gear.

I don't think I'm cool or smart, but I am caring, and I remember details. I am a good person and can be a good friend. I might look at getting into therapy so I can work on myself and my confidence.

🌍 🌍 🌍 Scene Five: Human Mercury

I get overwhelmed when a lot of people talk to me at once. I don't like strong smells but I can block them out if I focus hard and don't have other stress. When I'm triaging, social anxiety is the biggest issue, so if I can strategize for that, the rest is more manageable.

Aim: *Meet regularly in real life with a small group of friends who share a common interest.*

⬆ Successful? Sweeeeet! ⬇ Unsuccessful?
Re-evaluate or back down to repeat the steps.

⬆ Hold second meeting. Get feedback from group
– can we improve? Do they want to meet again?

⬆ Evaluate first meeting. Do we need more
space/resources/people/structure/etc.?

⬆ Hold initial test meeting.

⬆ Arrange logistics for first group meeting. → Date/
time/place. → Communicate (how/who?).

⬆ Discuss possibilities and details.

⬆ Make contact (prefer email if possible). → Propose
idea or suggest initial one-on-one meet up.

⬆ Research a connector to start with
(gaming, or maybe even biking?).

⬆

Go online and research NOW!

Energy In & Energy Out: I get energy connecting with certain people. I feel better after favourite bike ride. I get drained by logistical demands, and social rules and expectations that I don't understand.

The New World: I want to let go of my fear that I will always be an outsider. I want to own who I am and how I need the world to be. I want to be comfortable with exactly the way I am, and find people who understand and accept that.

☯ ☯ ☯ Scene Six: Energy and Fire

The gaming community feels good to me, I have had some good talks with others on game night. I had a conflict at the first one I went to, but that doesn't mean another time, another group, or another game can't feel right for me. I will keep trying different groups so I can figure out what works and doesn't work for me. I can learn and grow and find my people!

Big Picture: I want to have a small group of friends, work that I enjoy, and have the time and resources to bike awesome trails across the country. I think it would be good to live in a place where I have independence, but don't have to think about logistics like house maintenance or gardening. With my parents is good for now. When I'm ready, and have been working and saving for a while, I'd like to live somewhere in the city, so I can walk, bike, or bus to places I like to go (ideally near to a market, medical centre, library, or group meet-up). I think I'd like to work from home if I can, with data, so I can manage my energy and control the amount of people time I have.

I intend to be a good group member, listen to others at least as much as I talk (maybe more?), I want to appreciate other people, and also set and keep my own boundaries that help me feel safe. I intend to finish my qualifications and find an employment mentor so I can grow in experience and be good at my work. I intend to be consistent and reliable in my routine so I can feel safe enough to try new things personally. I intend to schedule times to reset and recharge, including biking regularly.

Fire! I really like gaming, biking, numbers, alone time. I want a life with more of these things in it!

🌐 🌐 🌐 Scene Seven: Autism-Friendly Is Human-Friendly

I like having music available, a dark space to myself. I've never tried commercial fidgets, but I have some little magnets that I like playing with, so I'm going to try buying some different things and see what works.

Universal Human: A standing/walking desk could work really well for me, maybe figure out ways to get in some activity breaks during gaming, or balance out gaming days with biking days. I'm going to look into mentoring for education/work, I think that could help me be more effective.

My Army: I have some online connections, it's great to have people to game with but not feel pressured to meet in real life. I have fun with them and can be myself without any sensory stuff. I collect movie character figurines, and having them around my computer makes me feel motivated. My family support me and are good people, but they don't really 'get' me. I'd like to connect with people like me. Ideally, build a small group of friends with a shared interest. Regular social contact in person would be good, but I need it to be structured so I can manage my overwhelm.

Get to the Yes: There's a gaming store in the city that I'd like to connect with. I can see if they have any gaming groups I can join, or if I can help set one up. (Maybe the biking community too?)

🌐 🌐 🌐 Scene Eight: The Bridge Builders

I find it easy to be the first one to break silence, to ease awkwardness, because I want people to be comfortable. I can help people who spend a lot of time online to move into real-life spaces.

I have always thought of myself as weird and wrong, but I'm autistic and that's kind of awesome. I want to explore more of the positives and use more strategies for my challenges. Like, I can schedule work to enjoy my high-energy hours. I can make sure I have more down time to recharge.

🌐 🌐 🌐 Scene Nine: The New World

The Glow: Gaming and biking make me feel the happiest. I also like the certainty of numbers.

Finding the Fuse:

I like disappearing into myself – either online, gaming, or biking. I like getting absorbed into my senses, it lets me feel free and less self-conscious.

Feeling the Fuse:

I feel less self-conscious and clunky, just immersed, light, and free. There's a feeling of space and air around my face. The rest of my body dissolves into that lightness and space.

Feeding the Fuse:

I have plenty of time allocated to being
online, I will plan more bike rides.

Firing the Fuse:

I will make playlists for the different routes.
Let myself feel the feeling more.

🌍 🌍 🌍 Scene Ten: Autistic World Domination

I will look out for
opportunities to be happy.

I am ready for anything!

The Rollercoaster

Hey autistics, in case no one's told you yet, all your feelings are valid. All of them. Not just the *autism pride*, but the *autism sucks*, too. Like the family that we love but know too well for rose-coloured glasses, autism is ours to feel about however we want. This section is to remind you, autistic to autistic, that for all the power and potential you have, you also have a right to be angry. To be sad. To be confused, ripped off, frustrated, and overwhelmed. Autism means feeling deeply, processing wildly, living intensely, diving into the seen and unseen with fresh skin and no choice about it. But the current world is designed by and for neurotypical brains. So, being autistic in this (current) world is intense. It is often hard, unfair, and exhausting. This is a space to acknowledge the trauma that stands alongside the joy.

It starts at the twinge of change. Alarms are going off. Maybe someone makes a comment, and you brush it off. At first. Maybe you see a character that resonates, read a book that clicks. Maybe it's someone else's diagnosis. A friend. A family member. Your child. So, you search the internet, and suddenly your head gets quiet: *Could I be autistic?*

You keep digging, hoping for something definitive. As you go through the info, the lists, the traits, you find yourself ticking them off, *that's me..., that's me..., that's me*. More and more falls into place. Your quirks, your routines. Maybe even your whole life.

I was diagnosed autistic as a grown-up. Way past the point where I could change the direction of my life, but perfectly timed to change the way I saw it.

I'm not here to tell you how to feel. There's no satisfaction in toxic positivity. I'm not going to pretend that being autistic is all yippy-skippy-superpowers. Don't get me wrong, autistic joy is powerful, and the upsides are epic. But mostly? Right now, being autistic hurts. It's overwhelming, frustrating, relentless, exhausting work in a world that sees us as broken.

You may not have a formal diagnosis; you may not have the words right now. You might feel lost, alone, and broken. Know this: You belong. You are wanted. You have a place in this world for the simple fact that you made it, you're here. You exist.

And the best part? You're not alone. Autistics are in every country, every industry, across genders, ages, and cultures. We are everywhere. Estimates now put the autistic population at 1 in 44 but that will still be low. Like me, an entire generation of autistics are discovering their neurodivergence as adults – either because they burn out after years of working to fit in, or when their children are diagnosed the process awakens their own truth. Autism has been called an epidemic, but what if it's a revolution? We're all out here, holding it together, holding it in so no one finds out 'what's wrong with us', when actually? It's the whole world that needs turning inside out.

I had all the advantages of growing up without an autistic label; no one told me what I couldn't do. But I also had all the disadvantages of growing up without an autistic identity, I didn't know who I was. Accepting my adult diagnosis and owning my identity has meant realizing how many life decisions I've made based on my belief that I was broken.

What would I have done differently if I had believed that I was designed specifically, perfectly, powerfully even? Eventually,

I realized that my weaknesses are strengths, and my strengths are superpowers. But only when I saw myself as exactly as I am.

I'm not special. I'm not the first, the best, or the last of my kind. I'm a baby in the world of autism. There is so much to learn. I only have my story to offer, but our stories can be so much more powerful than the statistics. They have to be. I'm grateful to follow the voices of those who came before me, and to put out a call for those who follow: We can be, do, or have anything.

Autistic adults

There are still people who consider autism a childhood issue, something they can train or educate away, a temporary state we grow out of. Guys, we don't grow out of it. If anything, we grow into it. We adapt, we modify, we change who we are. Many of us work incredibly hard to appear neurotypical and this is known as masking.

> Masking can include facial expressions, words, body language, even life choices (career, home, relationships, etc.). Masking is a survival mechanism, often unconscious. Ironically, the masking we do that keeps us from standing out in a neurotypical crowd is also why we tend to blend into a neurotypical crowd and miss out on diagnosis. Masking is one reason many neurodivergent people aren't found, diagnosed, or supported.

Masking is the ability to hide – or mask – autistic traits, shaping ourselves to fit into the regular world like a tribe of Clark Kents on Planet Earth. And it's not exactly conscious, although we do know we're doing it, it's a kind of survival skill, a camouflage.

Don't get me wrong; it's a mask but it's not fake, it's very real. More like a head than a mask, actually. And it's exhausting. It's like being 'on' all the time, working to be what the people around you expect to see. It's you, but holding your breath. Tweaked and refined and making an *effort* to keep up. And the sucky part? Even when we know we're doing it, it's not something we can just shut off. It wasn't a choice to start, and it's not as easy as just stopping. Because masking happens little by little, over time we learn to read the body language, play the social games, we figure out who we have to be so that people don't figure out that we're different. And because masking builds up bit by bit over our entire life, it's woven into our cells. It's speech patterns, habits, thoughts, it's very much *who we are*, and unmasking is not as simple as 'dropping the mask'. Unmasking is a process of relearning, reliving, rediscovering who we really are. It takes time, energy, and huge amounts of patience.

The thing about feeling different and not having a reason is you blame yourself. Clearly everyone else is coping with these perfectly normal human things. No one else is refusing to wear clothing because of itchy seams or scratchy tags. No one else is freaking out because the supermarket is so loud and bright and unpredictable. No one else is flinching at eye contact (although it kind of burns, like a bucketful of water being dumped on a sponge, or a speed-reader having an encyclopaedia flipped in their face). So, we pretend we're okay. We mask. If no one else is seeing or feeling or being hurt by these things, we must be wrong, right?

Trauma

A life lived this way – doubtful, displaced, disconnected – has a natural consequence: trauma. Even if you had a best-case scenario childhood, loving supportive family, a diagnosis and support, interests that were encouraged, a strong sense of self, you probably still heard yourself described as having a 'disorder'. And whether you register it consciously or not, you take on the language around you. Words have power.

And worst-case? Autistics are more likely to be bullied and hurt at home, at school, and in the workplace. We are more likely to be targets for abuse. Our sensitivity makes us vulnerable, and our isolation makes us less likely to ask for help. And even those of us who are brave enough to speak up are often ignored, disbelieved, or blamed.

It is an autism myth that we don't have empathy. Many autistics are attuned to the feelings of people, animals, plants, even inanimate objects. These rushes of emotion can be overwhelming and affect us all differently. Some autistics shut down to defend against overwhelm, others collect or keep objects they feel drawn to, some of us can read other people's emotions even before they do.

Some autistics can even develop hyper-empathy as a response to trauma. We learn that our survival depends on our ability to predict the emotions of the people around us. So, we work extra hard to understand and anticipate what other people need. Empathy can't always be judged from the outside. The intensity of our emotions (empathy included) is another reason we can be vulnerable.

If we want to protect autistics, we need to give them language, truth, and respect. We don't protect them by hiding the truth, or by pushing them to 'fit in'. We protect them by letting them know that their safety, comfort, and happiness matters. Abuse thrives in silence and denial.

When I was diagnosed with PTSD, my doctor explained to me that whether a trauma is experienced or witnessed, life-threatening, or perceived to be life-threatening, your brain and body reacts in the same way. That was key for me. My brain was trying to prove I was okay, but my body was telling a different story. The body remembers.

PTSD (post-traumatic stress disorder) can develop after a stressful event. Symptoms include reliving the trauma, hypervigilance, depression, anxiety, and avoidance strategies.

C-PTSD (complex post-traumatic stress disorder) can develop after exposure to long-term or repeated trauma. The symptoms can vary but include anger, negative thoughts, damaged relationships, and even somatic symptoms (such as nausea, fatigue, muscle pain, etc.).

The reasons why autistics are susceptible to trauma are the very same reasons we are exactly what the world needs. We bring honesty, innocence, vulnerability, sensitivity, justice. We are human. Autistically human. We carry with us the consequences of existing in a world that is hostile to different. And we deserve better. No more waiting to be caught, searching for a safe space, and holding our breath. We deserve to be here.

Diagnosis

Why get a diagnosis? Maybe it makes no difference – you've survived this long, kicked ass even. You don't want anything to change. You don't want or need to be treated differently. You reeeally don't want to get *the look*. But maybe? You could get affirmation, acknowledgement. You could give the people around you new ways to understand and support you. You could be okay with giving yourself a break. You've felt wrong for a long time, and maybe? This could mean feeling right.

A diagnosis is a journey. Recognizing the signs, navigating the system, getting the diagnosis, learning how the traits present for you, adjusting to the new world. This is not like an infection – you find it and fix it. This is a way of being in the world.

That's why, personally, I don't think a formal diagnosis is necessary, because environment is huge. For me, because I already felt so different, outside, and wrong – the diagnosis was a relief, it explained the ways I didn't fit. But (maybe) if I had felt more accepted in general, more certain of my strengths and my place on the planet, it never would have mattered why I was how I was. I would've just been me. And maybe that's what being on the spectrum really is, being completely you. (That's another reason I love the Māori word for autism (*takiwātanga*), it means in his or her own time and space, totally! Being beautifully yourself and doing things in exactly your own way.)

In the end? It doesn't matter why anyone chooses to get a diagnosis (or whether they even do), it's only important to know your why. Your why will let you know how hard to push, how far to go. It will keep you on track. Do you need evidence? A strong feeling? To be 50/50? Do you need a doctor's certificate?

If you're looking for a sense of identity, a way to describe your feelings, or affirmation, self-diagnosis can be enough. In the autistic community, self-diagnosis is totally valid and accepted. Formal diagnosis can be time-consuming, energy-draining, expensive, and (especially if you're female or gender diverse) difficult to achieve, so unfortunately still a privilege that is out of reach for many people. Groups of #ActuallyAutistics are usually open to members who are self-diagnosed or questioning. Happily, we really do seem to 'get' each other very quickly, so chances are, if you join a group and feel like you belong – you do! If you feel sure you are autistic, you're probably right. Lots of autistics are self-diagnosed, and it's often part of our autistic nature to research a diagnosis so thoroughly that we end up with as much (or more!) knowledge as the official 'experts'. But if you're looking to access government, medical, or educational support? To justify your feelings, explain who you are to friends, family, or workmates? To give it a name? To prove you're not overreacting? (Spoiler alert: You're not!) You might want to explore an official diagnosis.

Talk to your doctor, ask for a referral to a specialist. Remember: it's important to talk to medical professionals who understand the different ways autism can present. So don't be put off if the first doctor you talk to doesn't get it. Doctors can be amazing resources, but they're also just people, and we can forget that they don't know everything – and they definitely have some knowledge gaps here! Over the years, I've presented with lots of autistic traits and been diagnosed with lots of the peripheral conditions (major depressive disorder, anxiety disorder, all-around-awesomeness, etc.), and yet, a doctor familiar with women on the spectrum picked it up on my first visit. Autism can be so different across genders – and that's why it gets missed, because people are looking for the 'classic' signs, aka straight-cis-male signs, and not all autistics have them! Or, they have them, and they're interpreted differently. ('He doesn't make eye contact.' – 'Oh, he might be autistic!' 'She doesn't make eye contact.' – 'Oh, she's just shy with new people!')

Choosing to share your diagnosis (or not) is your decision. No one 'deserves' or is 'owed' access to your personal information. And (in case this isn't obvious) you should be treated with kindness and respect whether people know your diagnosis or not! Diagnosis is a beginning. You don't have to tell anyone, you don't have to keep it secret. Do what feels right for you. There is no script for 'coming out', no media to model on. Take time to process it, to decide what it means to you. Maybe a diagnosis won't change anything. Or maybe it will change everything.

You are not broken. You do not need to be fixed. You don't have to be diagnosed for your feelings to be 'real' and it is up to you whether you ever tell anyone. A diagnosis doesn't mean limits or restrictions; it just gives you information and choices. (It could even open up to who you are and how you can be happier in the world.)

The future: Autism without the disorder

If you're an autistic adult and you survive long enough, it's because you have strategies in place. Your world has been shaped around you. Perhaps deliberately (like food and clothing choices), perhaps accidentally (like the family or professionals who influence you), or perhaps fortuitously (like career and relationship pathways).

Whether you know you're neurodivergent or not, as an adult, you have more control over your world, and you mould it little by little. So, when or if you become a parent, that reshaped world is already in place for your children. And if your children are neurodivergent? They won't have the same levels of trauma and stress, because their environment is inherently autistic-friendly. For example: I've coped pretty well because I've set my life up to be super autistic-friendly (strong routines, work from home, as few people as possible, favourite foods on repeat, etc.). However, my autistic-friendly lifestyle has made it very hard for my children to be (officially) recognized as autistic.

When we first took our son in, looking for a diagnosis, I wanted confirmation of what my husband and I felt strongly, that he's autistic. Curious, sensitive, and innovative in so many amazing ways. But despite my believing, my *knowing* that self-diagnosis is completely valid, the brainwashed, colonized, needing-to-prove-myself parts of me wants to hear it from a traditionally recognized professional (whether they spend their nights reading the latest autism research, and whether I can already out-argue their outdated ideas or not).

Our ten-year-old son listened to the doctor list off the diagnostic criteria and all the ways he didn't meet them.

Does he have difficulties with social interaction? – No.

Does he have difficulties with communication? – No.

Does he have difficulties? – Not really.

The doctor was reluctant to diagnose him. She said, he clearly has autistic traits – hyperlexia, social differences, strong preferences, sensory sensitivities, absolute awesomeness – but he didn't meet the diagnostic criteria, because the official diagnosis requires evidence of deficits.

> Does he have difficulties with social interaction? – No, we enrolled him in a small school when he was nearly three years old. He's had the same friends and teachers for as long as he can remember. He's surrounded by people who – for the most part – know him and understand him.

> Does he have difficulties with communication? – No, we taught him sign language as a baby, he has a full-time autistic coach (his mother) and neuro navigator (his father). We talk a lot at our house, we give details, provide explanations. Home is our safe space. There are no surprises, food is negotiated, social interaction is followed by recovery. We tell him that other people think differently to us sometimes, and that's okay. We teach him to be patient with people who have different wiring.

> Does he have difficulties? – Not really. It's not perfect, we're all still learning, but he's not shutting down, melting down, or acting out. The doctor can't tick any of the boxes she needs to tick.

In the car on the way home, our son was quiet for a while. He listened as we explained that even though he clearly has a lot of autistic traits, the doctors only use problems to officially define autism.

Then our son said, 'It's simple. Can't I just be autistic without the disorder?'

Stunned silence. Beautiful truth. And that's the future. Not having your identity determined by what you can't do, and how you don't measure up. Autism without the disorder. Autistics raised in autism-friendly environments, untraumatized autistics. A future where we get to have both – the identity and the understanding.

Disclaimer: I'm not a doctor, not a formally qualified expert, I'm *tangata whaitakiwātanga*, an autistic person. Autistics are individuals – surprise! And I can only, and do only, speak for myself. If you know an autistic, talk to them! (Unless they don't like that, then write them an email.) Because seriously, we need all the voices, all the stories, all the optimism we can get. Growing up, I didn't know anyone who was openly neurodivergent. It didn't occur to me that I might just be different, not broken or wrong. They say you can't be what you can't see, right? I speak up, because we need at least as many autistic points of view - with words, without words, signing, typing, singing, screaming, eye rolling, sarcastic, angry, authentic autistic points of view – as there currently are neurotypicals telling our stories.

Heoi anō, here we go...

So that's it! If you're an autistic finding your place, or a neurotypical supporting the process; *Autistic World Domination* is your secret handshake, your invitation, your ticket in. Welcome to the new world! Not only do you belong here, but you are part of making it happen. Take what works, leave what doesn't, and know that when you create a world that works perfectly for you, it ripples out and benefits everyone. Are you ready? Take a breath, take your time, this is going to be awesome. Let's rewrite normal!

Whakataukī (Māori proverbs)

A rock in the ocean. *Te toka tū moana.*

Bravery has many resting places. *He toa taumata rau.*

The tītoki tree blooms in its own time. *He wā tōna ka puāwai mai te tītoki.*

The legs of the rainbow stand in two different places. *Āniwaniwa tū wae rua.*

There is one Spirit that flows through all. *Kotahi tonu te Wairua o nga mea katoa.*

One cannot know from the outside what is contained within. *E mōhiotia ana a waho kei roto he ana.*

Words have power. *He mana tō te kupu.*

Endnotes

1   Guan, J. and Li, G. (2017) Injury mortality in individuals with autism. *American Journal of Public Health, 107*, 791–793. doi:10.2105/AJPH.2017.303696

2   Singer, J. (2020, 12 August) What is wrong with this Wikipedia definition of neurodiversity? [Blog post]. Reflections on Neurodiversity. https://neurodiversity2.blogspot.com/2020/08

3   Kassiane Asasumasu is a multiply neurodivergent Hapa (biracial Asian) neurodiversity activist. Read more at: www.divergentminds.org/our-team

4   Shuker, K. (2001) *The Hidden Powers of Animals*. Reader's Digest. Also cited at https://asknature.org/strategy/feet-sensitive-to-sweetness

5   Weldon, L.Z. (n.d.) On the neurodivergent majority. www.weldonwellness.com/posts/neurodivergent-majority

6   University of Montreal (2009, 17 June) Autistics better at problem-solving, study finds. *ScienceDaily*. www.sciencedaily.com/releases/2009/06/090616121339.htm

7   Markowsky, G. (n.d.) Information Theory. *Encyclopedia Britannica*. www.britannica.com/science/information-theory/Physiology

8   Cusack, J. (2021, 18 February) Autistic people still face highest rates of unemployment of all disabled groups. Autistica. www.autistica.org.uk/news/autistic-people-highest-unemployment-rates

9   Lewis, T.A. (2022, 1 January) Working definition of Ableism – January 2022 update [Blog post]. www.talilalewis.com/blog

10 Crenshaw, K. (2017) Kimberlé Crenshaw on intersectionality, more than two decades later [Interview]. Columbia Law School. www.law.columbia.edu/news/archive/kimberle-crenshaw-intersectionality-more-two-decades-later

11 Milton, D.E.M. (2012) On the ontological status of autism: The 'double empathy problem'. *Disability & Society, 27*(6), 883–887.

12 Morgan, K. (2011, 14 June) Heeding the taniwha can help avert expensive blunders. *NZ Herald*. www.nzherald.co.nz/kahu/kepa-morgan-heeding-the-taniwha-can-help-avert-expensive-blunders/VNSRYM7XFPJA67HMNNZHHZ6TPI